Tricia B. Bent-Goodley, PhD, MSW
Editor

African-American Social Workers and Social Policy

Pre-publication
REVIEWS,
COMMENTARIES,
EVALUATIONS . . .

"Few books in social work have examined the specific dilemmas and challenges of American social policy among African Americans. Bent-Goodley significantly fills this often neglected literature gap by offering a comprehensive and diverse analysis of important social policy issues that confront African Americans. This book is a must-read for students, professors, and policy practitioners who seek an African-American perspective of social policy analysis and advocacy."

Jerome H. Schiele, DSW
Professor, The Ethelyn R. Strong
School of Social Work,
Norfolk State University;
Author, *Human Services
and the Afrocentric Paradigm*

"*African-American Social Workers and Social Policy* provides perspectives that are driven by an understanding of the needs of the black community and directions for social change. Written by scholars and activists who have struggled with the dilemma of serving clients, government, and specific communities whose interest may diverge, the book examines participation in social change and specific policy issues such as Social Security, TANF, kinship care, mental health, and child welfare. The contributors use the most recent data to describe the policy challenges confronting African Americans. This book is a critical resource at a time when policy changes being contemplated may place African Americans at greater risk. All social workers who care about African Americans should read this book. And further, anyone who cares about creating community in America should read this book."

Carol Wilson Spigner, DSW
Kenneth L. Pray Distinguished Professor,
University of Pennsylvania

The Haworth Social Work Practice Press
An Imprint of The Haworth Press, Inc.
New York • London • Oxford

African-American Social Workers and Social Policy

THE HAWORTH SOCIAL WORK PRACTICE PRESS
Social Work Practice in Action
Carlton E. Munson
Senior Editor

Human Behavior in the Social Environment: Interweaving the Inner and Outer World by Esther Urdang

Family Health Social Work Practice: A Knowledge and Skills Casebook edited by Francis K. O. Yuen, Gregory J. Skibinski, and John T. Pardeck

African-American Social Workers and Social Policy edited by Tricia B. Bent-Goodley

The Social Work Student's Research Handbook byDominique Moyse Steinberg

African-American Social Workers and Social Policy

Tricia B. Bent-Goodley, PhD, MSW
Editor

The Haworth Social Work Practice Press
An Imprint of The Haworth Press, Inc.
New York • London • Oxford

Published by

The Haworth Social Work Practice Press, an imprint of The Haworth Press, Inc., 10 Alice Street, Binghamton, NY 13904-1580.

Cover design by Brooke Stiles.

Cover logo illustration, *African-Family Capital,* copyright 2003 by Angela E. Sussewell.

Library of Congress Cataloging-in-Publication Data

African-American social workers and social policy / Tricia Bent-Goodley, editor.
    p. cm.
    An outgrowth of a June 2000 summit of African American social workers funded by the Howard University Fund for Academic Excellence.
    Includes bibliographical references and index.
    ISBN 0-7890-1621-4 (hard : alk. paper)—ISBN 0-7890-1622-2 (soft : alk. paper)
    1. African American social workers. 2. United States—Social policy—1993—Evaluation. 3. African Americans—Social conditions—21st century. 4. Social work with African Americans. I. Bent-Goodley, Tricia B.

HV3181 .A374 2003
362.84'96'073—dc21

    2002027333

CONTENTS

ABOUT THE EDITOR

Tricia B. Bent-Goodley, PhD, MSW, is the Immediate Past Chair of the NABSW National Public Policy Institute and Immediate Past Chair and Chief Instructor of the NABSW National Academy for African-Centered Social Work. She has organized local communities and grassroots organizations to engage in political networking, local and state advocacy, policy agenda setting, policy forums, and political candidate debates. She has organized national training and education for social workers in social policy, policy analysis, and policy advocacy. Dr. Bent-Goodley has served as a clinician, program planner, supervisor, administrator, and entrepreneur. She has co-edited two forthcoming books with Dr. King E. Davis, titled *The Color of Social Policy* and *Teaching Social Policy in Social Work Education.*

Contributors

Sandra Stukes Chipungu, PhD, is Associate Professor at Howard University School of Social Work. She holds her MSW and PhD from the University of Michigan. Dr. Chipungu is a co-editor of and contributor to *Child Welfare: An Africentric Perspective* (Rutgers University Press, 1997). She teaches Theories of Administration in the PhD program, and Management in Human Services, Social Welfare Policy, Policy Practice, and Family and Child Welfare I and II in the MSW Program. Her current research focuses on child welfare, foster care, kinship care, evaluation of services to substance-using pregnant and postpartum women, and high-risk youth.

Shelia L. Clark, MSW, is Project Manager for the Partners in Program Planning for Adolescent Health (PIPPAH) initiative at the National Association of Social Workers (NASW) and former Public Policy Associate for the National Black Women's Health Project. In her current position, she focuses on the development and implementation of strategies to promote adolescent health. She currently serves on the Board of Directors for My Sister's Place shelter for battered women and the Reproductive Health Technologies Project. She is also a member of the Black Church Initiative Advisory Committee.

Sandra Edmonds Crewe, PhD, MSW, ACSW, received her BSW and MSW from the National Catholic School of Social Services and a PhD in Social Work from Howard University. Currently, she is an Assistant Professor at the Howard University School of Social Work and teaches research, macro practice, and social gerontology. Dr. Crewe has been the principal investigator of research and evaluations on welfare reform since 1994. In addition, she serves on the professional development faculty of the National Association of Housing and Redevelopment Officials where she leads seminars across the country for resident leaders in public and assisted housing. Dr. Crewe serves on the boards of the National Association of Social Workers (Washington DC Metro Chapter) and the United Communities Against Poverty in Prince George's County, Maryland.

King E. Davis, PhD, holds the Robert Lee Sutherland Chair in Mental Health and Social Policy at the University of Texas at Austin, School of Social Work. Dr. Davis was a Professor of Public Mental Health Policy and Planning at the Virginia Commonwealth University School of Social Work from 1984 to 2000. From 1998 to 1999, he was the holder of the William and Camille Cosby Chair at Howard University's School of Social Work, Washington, DC. Also in 1999, King was appointed to the Libra Chair at the University of Maine, and was a Distinguished Visiting Professor at Washington University in St. Louis. He was awarded the PhD from the Florence G. Heller School of Social Policy and Management at Brandeis University in 1971. His doctoral work focused on the financing of nonprofit organizations.

Dr. Davis is a former Commissioner of the Virginia Department of Mental Health, Mental Retardation, and Substance Abuse Services, appointed by L. Douglas Wilder, Governor of Virginia, and served from 1990 to 1994.

Wilhelmina A. Leigh, PhD, is a Senior Research Associate at the Joint Center for Political and Economic Studies in Washington, DC. She is an economist who has worked in the following areas: health policy, housing policy, labor market issues, and social insurance. Recent publications about social insurance include: *Social Security: A Fix for All* and the issue brief *Social Security Reform: What Proposed Changes Mean for African Americans.* Dr. Leigh received her PhD in Economics from Johns Hopkins University and her AB, also in Economics, from Cornell University.

Preface

The impetus for this book was listening to the lyrics of Tupac Shakur. He states in one of his songs, "Changes," "I'm tired of being poor and even worse I'm black. . . . We gotta start making changes. Learn to see me as your brother instead of two distant strangers." These two lines had a great impact on me but what stood out even more was the eloquence with which he spoke about the pervasiveness of poverty, the viciousness of police brutality, the consequences of feeling powerless to change the environment, and the feeling that he was in this alone. As I listened to other rap artists share their life stories, it became evident that as one examined the lyrics beyond the vulgarity, there was a distinct message concerning social policy. Tupac is one example; however, many of these young people talk about welfare, stereotypes of African Americans, poverty, police corruption, the role of substance abuse, and policies that support these problems. As I sat listening to his words that day, I thought about the young people who I provide services for as a social worker. Their feelings of hopelessness to influence change or policy were clear to me. I thought of previous generations that believed they could create change and did so, in large part, because they believed that they could. What about this generation of young people? Who is their voice? How can we move beyond the language and the violence to hear what is a clear message for action? For me, policy is clearly linked to young people. Thus, I decided to move beyond the rhetoric to find creative ways of influencing social policy and helping others to empower themselves in this arena.

In June 2000, African-American social workers and scholars came together for a policy summit solely focused on addressing policy issues relevant to African Americans. The policy summit was funded by the Howard University Fund for Academic Excellence. This book is an outgrowth of the summit. It is our hope that the book will provide professionals and students from social work and other disciplines with the opportunity to hear the voices of African Americans on important policy issues and to help them understand the complexity of social policy from a diverse perspective. Many social welfare policy texts are written by individuals who do not speak to the experiences of people of color. Until people of color can create a policy agenda that fits within the diversity of each group it will be extremely challenging to engage in the kind of coalition building that can reflect a collective effort across groups. *The Color of Social Policy,* an additional book edited by myself and King E. Davis, will further the discussion in this area.

Communities of African ancestry are in dire need of leadership from social work professionals in the policy arena. We must not only be a voice in the policy process but we must also be a force toward social change for ourselves and humanity.

Acknowledgments

This book has been a collective effort from the very beginning. I would like to thank each of my colleagues for their timeliness, detail, and support of this project from the onset. This book would not have been possible without the financial support of the Howard University Office of the Provost that funded the policy summit and research on African-American social workers and social policy. Many thanks to all in the Office of Research Administration who support the project, particularly Ann Collymore, Leonard Clay, and S. Terrie Bowen. I would also like to thank my colleagues at Howard University School of Social Work and the National Association of Black Social Workers for their guidance and support. Thanks to my students who force me to strive for perfection. Many thanks to the Advisory Committee for the summit that helped formulate the agenda: Dr. Robert E. Fullilove, Leonard G. Dunston, G. Rosaline Preudhomme, Dr. Lawrence E. Gary, and Dr. Carol Wilson-Spigner. A special thanks to my role models that continue to inspire me through mentorship and friendship: Dr. Iris B. Carlton-LaNey and Dr. King E. Davis. I am eternally in debt to the two of you. I would also like to thank my sisters of Alpha Kappa Alpha Sorority, Inc. for implanting the vision for this work and allowing me to grow in skill through service. I am grateful to my former clients and staff who taught me so much about what you will read in this book.

I would also like to thank my friends and family who withstood my focus on this project and others. Thank you for continuing to love and support me despite myself. I would like to particularly thank Lauren Francis and Dr. Gladys Hall for editorial support. Many thanks to my sister, Kim E. Adams, for always being willing to listen. I would also like to thank my brothers for their support: Trevor S. Bent, Gary Bent, and Calvin C. Bent, II, and my sisters-in-law, Carla and Cathi. My nieces and nephews continue to motivate me to do better and be better: Michael Bent, Troy Turner, Tricia S. Bent, Carolyn C. Adams, Melanie R. Adams, Calvin C. Bent III, Carl M. Bent, and Kirsten A. Bent.

Thanks to my mother for always believing in me and supporting me. She is the reason I am who I am. It is because of her character and sacrifice that I am here today. I also thank my father for his ancestral support. I thank him for instilling in me a sense of pride and victory. For this reason, this book is dedicated to the two of you: Nellie F. Bent and Calvin C. Bent I. This book was largely written and edited with my sleeping infant in the nook of my left arm. My son, Malcolm, has been an inspiration for me to be a better person and make a real contribution through my work. He is my absolute greatest joy. My husband is my backbone, a pillar of strength, my greatest motivator, and the one who knows me the best and loves me anyway. I am grateful to my husband for always believing in me, especially when I stop believing in myself. Marvin, from the depths of my soul, thank you. Finally, I thank the Creator for continuing to allow me to do this work and for blessing me with ability, support, and strength to move forward. Without Him, there would be nothing.

Chapter 1

The Role of African-American Social Workers in Social Policy

Policy practice can be defined as "efforts to change policies in legislative, agency and community settings, whether by establishing new policies, improving existing ones, or defeating the policy initiatives of other people" (Jansson, 1999, p. 10). The Council on Social Work Education (CSWE) Educational Policy and Accreditation Standards (EPAS) (2001) has reinforced the need for a greater emphasis on policy practice in educating social work students. The value of policy practice has been emphasized as significant for all social workers in impacting key social work issues (Figueira-McDonough, 1993; Haynes and Mickelson, 2000; Jansson, 1999; Schneider and Lester, 2001). Social workers have been encouraged to impact social policy and use their unique role to lobby for social welfare policy that meets the needs of constituents (Domanski, 1998; Hoechstetter, 1996; Hoechstetter, 2001; Schneider and Netting, 1999; Stuart, 1999). Numerous publications provide specific techniques of political intervention, advocacy, and strategies to increase policy practice skill (Dear and Patti, 1981; Fisher, 1995; Jansson, 1999; Mahaffey and Hanks, 1982; Powell and Causby, 1994; Roberts-DeGennaro, 1986; Rocha, 2000; Schneider and Lester, 2001; Wolk et al., 1996). Much of the emphasis has been placed on increasing the motivation and desire of social workers to want to impact social change through enhanced political participation (Domanski, 1998; Ezell, 1993), yet it is unclear how African-American social workers perceive themselves within policy practice. As African Americans are disproportionately af-

The author thanks the National Association of Black Social Workers for its support of this study.

fected by social policy issues, such as child welfare (Brown and Bailey-Etta, 1997; Everett, Chipungu, and Leashore, 1997), it is important to assess their participation in social change through policy practice.

The role of African-American social welfare pioneers in policy practice has been illustrated (Bent-Goodley, 2001; Carlton-LaNey, 1994, 2001; Carlton-LaNey and Burwell, 1996) through activities such as lobbying, engaging in coalition building, developing relationships with policymakers, analyzing policy, organizing letter writing campaigns, and running for public office. Policy practice of contemporary African-American social workers has not been well documented. The purpose of this chapter is to report the findings of an exploratory study that examines the political participation and policy analysis criteria of African-American social workers.

LITERATURE REVIEW

Political participation can be defined as one's desire "to influence the structure of government, the selection of government authorities, or the policies of government" (Conway, 1991, p. 3). Previous studies on the political participation of social workers have either had small samples of African Americans or have provided limited attention and documentation of data analyzed according to race (Ezell, 1993; Hamilton and Fauri, 2001; Salcido and Seck, 1992). In addition, the study will examine the policy analysis criteria for African-American social workers. Policy analysis is defined as the development of "policy alternatives to address [policy issues], then select a preferred alternative in the course of policy deliberations" (Jansson, 2000, p. 41). The means by which African-American social workers evaluate social policies is also limited in the literature. This study seeks to build on both determining African-American social workers' political participation and understanding the ways in which African-American social workers assess policy.

Wolk's (1981) study of the political participation of social workers found that older social workers, those in macro positions, social workers with higher incomes, and those practicing in the profession longer were more likely to engage in political activity. Although he focused on those statistically significant findings, he also shared nonstatistically significant results that indicated a greater level of political participation by women than men, African Americans than whites, and social workers with doctorates versus those without doctorates. His findings did not illustrate the techniques of African-American social workers in impacting the policy process but it did acknowledge their higher level of political participation.

Salcido and Seck (1992) examined the political participation of fifty-two National Association of Social Work (NASW) chapters across the country. The study found that social workers were more likely to engage in writing letters, phoning officials, and lobbying legislators versus working with interest groups, campaigning, or organizing protest rallies, regarded as more conflict-oriented activities. Salcido and Seck further noted that "involvement in protest activities and voter registration is minimal" and that "these activities can be used to empower the poor, [people of color], and social service clients" (1992, p. 564). This study did not illustrate an examination of political participation according to race; however, it importantly noted that social workers are more likely to engage in political activities that are less confrontational, less rooted in grassroot communities, and less likely to be on behalf of and working with the oppressed.

Ezell (1993) examined the political participation of 353 members of the NASW Washington State Chapter (n = 311) and graduates of the University of Washington School of Social Work (n = 42). He found that "Black social workers [were] the most active; NASW members [were] more active than non-members and macro practitioners [were] more involved than micro practitioners" (p. 86). No statistical significance according to gender was found, although women appeared to be more politically active than men. It was the sample's previous volunteer experience that predicated the likelihood of greater political activity, although social workers were likely to engage in client advocacy more regularly than other types of influence. The study also found that social workers were more likely to engage in letter writing, attending meetings, and discussing politics among individual cohorts than campaigning, making contributions, and testifying. Finally, Ezell emphasizes the need to further expose social work students to political practice and to create a better understanding of how social work values and ethics can be integrated with the policy process.

Hamilton and Fauri (2001) reported on a survey that measured the political activity of 242 social workers in New York State. The findings confirmed no difference in political activity based on demographics such as income, upbringing, or age. However, they did find that those social workers most likely to engage in political activity were recruited to participate by an organization or were individuals already interested in political affairs.

These studies provide an important understanding of the political participation of social workers; however, the contributions and techniques of African-American social workers are not clearly delineated. As a result, this study built on the previous literature by enhancing our understanding of African-American social workers' role in the policy process.

Schiele (2000) promotes an African-centered approach to policy that includes race specific policies focused on improving the sociopolitical and economic standing of people of African ancestry. He emphasizes that policy analysis should be "understood more holistically and circularly in a manner that synthesizes seemingly contradictory and unrelated components" (p. 172). Understanding the strengths and self-help tradition of communities of African ancestry and including them in the policy decision-making process is a key aspect to analyzing social policy from an African-centered perspective. He further emphasizes the need to build on the collective standing of the community as opposed to using policy analysis to further oppress individuals and communities. Schiele provides a key understanding as to how one can use the policy process to empower people of African ancestry. This chapter will build on his work by identifying the means by which African-American social workers evaluate social policy.

METHODOLOGY

This study builds on the previous literature by focusing on the political participation of African-American social workers and their criteria for assessing social policy. A pilot study was conducted before the survey was disseminated to assess its reliability. A focus group was conducted with five African-American policy experts, including two policy practitioners on the state and federal levels respectively and three social policy scholars. The focus was to provide feedback on the questionnaire. Minor changes were made to the questionnaire as a result of the feedback.

Participants and Procedure

A purposive sample of 116 African-American social workers self-selected to participate in the survey utilizing a ten-item, closed-ended and seven-item, open-ended questionnaire. The study's participants were attending a policy workshop at the 2000 National Association of Black Social Workers (NABSW) Conference. There was a pool of 132 social workers at the session, indicating an 88 percent response rate.

The questionnaire consisted of three sections: the first section obtained demographic information, the second section obtained information regarding political participation and levels of influence, and the third section contained information on policy analysis criteria. To determine the primary methods of political activities and the extent of political participation, the respondents were asked to specify their methods of participation in ten political activities over the past two years. They also were asked to indicate additional methods of influence not listed. This process resulted in one additional category: voter registration and education or grassroots organizing. Level of political activity was gauged through self-identification on a scale of no or little participation as nonactive participation, occasional participation as active, and frequent participation as very active (Ezell, 1993).

The sample was predominantly composed of women, as 81 percent of respondents were female (n = 94). The age range of respondents was 23 years (n = 5) to 87 years (n = 2), a mean age of 42 years and a median age of 42.5 years. Thirty-four percent identified as direct service practitioners, 24 percent as macro practitioners, and 38 percent identified as using a combination of both areas of practice. Macro practitioners included supervisors, administrators, policy analysts, entrepreneurs, and community organizers. Ninety-four percent of respondents possessed a MSW degree, with 13 percent (n = 15) of respondents indicating a doctorate in social work.

FINDINGS

One quarter of respondents classified their political participation as nonactive, 55 percent as active, and 16 percent as very active. Respondents indicated that their greatest influence took place on the local level (56 percent, n = 65). The next greater area of influence took place on the state level (17 percent, n = 20), with the smallest amount of influence noted on the federal level (5.2 percent, n = 6).

Table 1.1 reveals the distribution of political activity among the respondents. Fifty percent of the respondents indicated working with interest groups to influence policy. Over one-third of respondents indicated the use of three types of political activities: voter registration and grassroots organizing (41 percent, n = 48), attending hearings (38 percent, n = 44), and engaging in letter writing campaigns (32 percent, n = 37).

One quarter or slightly less of respondents indicated the political activities of five methods: phoning officials (27 percent, n = 31), attending protest rallies (25 percent, n = 29), building interpersonal relationships with legislators (25 percent, n = 29), testifying (22 percent, n = 25), and lobbying officials (21 percent, n = 24). The lowest scores of political activities included participating in campaign activities

TABLE 1.1. Itemized Responses to Political Activity Methods of Influence

Item	Percentage	Number
Interest Groups and Coalitions	50	n = 58
Voter Registration and Education	41	n = 48
Attending Hearings	38	n = 44
Letter-Writing Campaigns	32	n = 37
Phone Calls	27	n = 31
Rally Participation	25	n = 29
Building Interpersonal Relationships with Legislators	25	n = 29
Testifying	22	n = 26
Lobbying Officials	21	n = 24
Campaigning	15	n = 17
Fundraising and Campaign Contributions	6	n = 7

(15 percent, n = 17) and contributing funds to campaigns (6 percent, n = 7).

Over 51 percent (n = 60) of the respondents indicated that their major reason for being involved in policy advocacy is because of a desire to fight racism and oppressive policies. The major policy issues identified as reasons for engaging in policy advocacy included to impact child welfare (47 percent, n = 55), criminal justice (25 percent, n = 30), welfare reform (18 percent, n = 21), and advocating against social work licensure (12 percent, n = 15).

Criteria for Policy Analysis

The following list reveals ten criteria for policy analysis as identified by the respondents.

1. Weigh the costs, trade-offs, benefits, and risks to communities of African ancestry.
2. Review existing knowledge and research.
3. Analyze the short- and long-term consequences to African Americans.
4. Talk to frontline workers.
5. Secure legal interpretations.
6. Ask for input by those most impacted.
7. Look for gaps by examining the depth and breadth of policy.
8. Policy analysis should be based on equity.
9. Policy analysis should consider the realities of implementation.
10. Investigate the background of sponsors and monetary contributors.

Respondents shared their responses to the question "When a policy is proposed, how do you analyze whether you will support the policy?" Their open-ended responses were analyzed using a content analysis and grouped according to ten identified themes.

Weigh the Costs

The greatest percentage of respondents indicated the need to "weigh the costs, trade-offs, benefits, and risks to communities of African ancestry." The need to understand the possible negative impact of a policy on the population was emphasized. It was clear that policies should be examined for how they impact the community and what one will have to give up in order for the intended policy to be implemented should be identified.

Review Existing Knowledge and Research

Respondents stressed the need to "review existing knowledge and research" before forming an opinion on a policy. It was emphasized that one should read all documentation before attempting to analyze a policy issue. This process provides a basis for fully understanding a policy instead of having others inform one's opinion.

Short- and Long-Term Consequences

The next criteria for analyzing policy includes conducting an "analysis of the short- and long-term consequences" of policy on communities of African ancestry. It was emphasized that this criterion is critical to understanding the full impact of a policy on the community.

Talk with Frontline Workers

Respondents emphasized the need to "talk with frontline workers." Understanding that frontline or direct service workers greatly impact policy implementation, respondents emphasized the importance of engaging the direct service worker from the outset (Jansson, 1999; Stuart, 1999). As opposed to engaging direct service workers after policy is formulated, one should include their perspective in the initial analysis. Respondents emphasized that the cooperation of frontline workers could help to ensure effective policy implementation.

Secure Legal Interpretations

Respondents indicated the need to "secure legal interpretations" as important for understanding the legal ramifications, options, and loopholes during the conducting of a comprehensive analysis. The emphasis was on using lawyers to provide legal analysis, not to conduct the analysis itself.

Asking for Input by Those Most Impacted

It was indicated that policy analysis should "ask for input by those most impacted." This criterion was recommended to include clients and grassroot community members from the beginning as opposed to surveying them at the end. Feeling that the policy process is often disconnected from community members, respondents identified the need to fully engage community members in the decision-making and policy analysis process.

Examine the Depth and Breadth

Respondents specified the need to look for gaps by "examining the depth and breadth" of policy. They indicated that policy analysis should include a comprehensive focus as opposed to a narrow examination.

Analysis Based on Equity

Policy analysis should be "based on equity." Policies should be assessed with a focus on fairness and securing equality as the primary objective. As opposed to creating race-based policy, the respondents advocated for equality-based policy.

Realities of Implementation

Policy analysis should take the "realities of implementation" into account. Without understanding the strengths and limitations within policy implementation, one could institute a policy that is not realistic. Thus policy analysis also should take the realities of implementation into account in order to be effective.

Investigate the Background of Key Sponsors and Monetary Contributors

The tenth criterion was to "investigate the background of key sponsors of legislation and monetary contributors." This criterion was stated as important to understanding and assessing policy, as the values of the sponsor and contributor are seen as inextricably tied to the policy making process (Gibbs and Bankhead, 2001). Respondents believed that if one understands the sponsor and those that are funding a particular policy, then one can better assess the motivation and focus of the policy.

DISCUSSION

Although this study focused on attempting to uncover the political participation and policy analysis criteria of African-American social workers, the findings provide important documentation of how African-American social workers engage in policy practice. Even though the findings are important, the limitations of the study must also be acknowledged.

Limitations

The first limitation of this project was that the respondents were voluntarily attending a policy workshop. It is possible that these individuals were already interested in policy, thus influencing their responses. The second limitation was that there was no qualitative component to the study that could have provided greater clarity of the survey responses. A focus group would have allowed for greater substantiation of why various activities were selected and why different policy analysis criteria were identified.

Level of Political Participation

Although 75 percent of the respondents indicated active to very active status of political participation, one quarter of the respondents indicated a nonactive status. Understanding the disproportionate manner in which African Americans are impacted by many of today's most compelling social issues, a need exists for all African-American social workers to participate, on some level, in policy practice. Comparatively, Salcido and Seck (1992) and Ezell (1993) found a nonactive level of 35 percent and 14.5 percent respectively. While 25 percent in the not active status category is in the middle of these two scores, there is still a need to better understand why one quarter of those surveyed indicated a nonactive status. Simultaneously, the fact that 75 percent of the respondents were either active or very active in political participation is notable.

Consensus- and Conflict-Oriented Approaches

Salcido and Seck (1992) found that social workers have been more likely to engage in consensus-oriented approaches, such as phoning legislators and face-to-face lobbying, than conflict-oriented approaches, such as voter registration and rallying. The respondents were less likely to engage in consensus-oriented approaches and demonstrated mixed responses in conflict-oriented approaches. The second largest political activity identified was voter registration. Many of the respondents likened this activity to grassroots organizing. One quarter of the participants engaged in rallying activities. It is unclear why these respondents were less likely to engage in consensus building approaches as opposed to conflict-oriented approaches. Respondents were less likely to influence the policy process on the federal and state levels. As one moves outside of the local community, there may be less familiarity and opportunities to engage public officials. This area warrants greater study.

Policy Assessment

The responses were clear in delineating that policy analysis does not take place in a linear fashion but includes critical components for assessment. This assertion is similar to Schiele's (2000) notion of the circular process of policy analysis. The two major criteria emphasized were the ability to weigh the impact of social policy on African Americans and to identify the sponsors and financial contributors of social policy. The major focus was on using policy analysis to create realistic policies that will be effective, provide equal treatment for people of African ancestry and other people of color, and ensure a positive impact for people of African ancestry on both a short- and long-term basis.

IMPLICATIONS

There are several implications for this study. African Americans do engage in political activities and appear to engage in such activities more comfortably through interest groups and grassroots organizing in the form of voter's registration. They are less likely to engage in political activity with policy makers. They also are less likely to influence policy on the state and federal level.

The Need for More Research

Greater research needs to be conducted to understand why African Americans use particular types of political activities more often than others. It is unclear if African Americans are more likely to engage in grassroots organizing through voter registration due to greater familiarity with such communities or if they are less likely to attempt to directly impact policy officials due to feeling less connected with state and federal officials who are often less likely to reflect the needs and beliefs of a particular community.

The Need for a Policy Agenda

African-American social workers appear to be motivated primarily by the need to fight racist and oppressive policies. Although they come together primarily concerning issues of child welfare, criminal justice, and welfare reform legislation, it is critical to formalize a policy agenda that provides focus and direction to these efforts. A formal agenda is particularly important as African-American social workers indicate a great amount of participation in interest groups. If these organizations are more politically active, targeted in their efforts, and integrated in their approaches, it is possible that African-American social workers would demonstrate a greater degree of political activity and influence. Although communities of African ancestry are diverse, their advocacy organizations need to assemble a core policy agenda and collectively work to create change across disciplines, religions, and types of organizations.

Greater Political Training

Organizations can also provide greater political training particularly as it relates to state and federal politics, lobbying techniques, and providing testimony regarding bills or issues. Although social work education has been encouraged to be more responsive in this area, African-American organizations have an even greater stake in social policy. Those Historically Black Colleges and Universities (HBCUs), particularly those with social work programs and African-American social welfare organizations, should work toward solidifying policy internships with a focus on state and federal levels. Such internships should not only be organized for BSW and MSW-level students but also should include post-doctoral opportunities. Field internships can also be organized in the policy arena with African-American social workers serving as field instructors where there are no social workers at the field site. Political training is not limited to institutes, conferences, and other workshops. Such institutions can also provide advanced training on other forms of advocacy from the direct service level to the macro level.

Making Policy Analysis Public

This study documents that African-American social workers engage in policy analysis. Such policy analysis should be published and presented to provide diverse perspectives of social policy (Davis and Bent-Goodley, in press). Without such information, the voice of African Americans will continue to not be heard. It is critical that African-American social workers not just analyze policy but publish and promote their positions. This type of advocacy is critical to providing justification for those African-American and other legislators with similar positions. Position papers, fact sheets, written testimony, and issue analyses can be sent to policymakers and implementers to persuade the reader to consider a new position.

Redefine African-American Scholarship

Much has gone into the definition of scholarship in the highly competitive academic environment. The role of using one's scholarship and position to advocate for equality and opportunity is no longer a criteria or emphasis for scholarship. Receiving grants and publishing in peer-reviewed journals seems to have replaced the emphasis on African-American scholars playing an important role in influencing public policy. Using examples of African-American social welfare pioneers, such as W. E. B. DuBois and Elizabeth Ross Haynes, and contemporary activists such as Cornel West and Mary Berry, African-American scholars need to use their scholarship to inform a political stance. Although developing theory and knowledge is critical, it is also important to use that information to, in some way, advance the position of African Americans and other people of color.

CONCLUSION

This chapter sought to understand the political participation of African-American social workers and to identify their criteria for analyzing social policy. The findings point to the need to create greater political influence on federal and state levels and to better understand the extent and nature of political participation of social workers of African ancestry. The study further points to the manner in which African Americans methodically analyze social policy. African-American social workers are taking important steps to use the policy process to create change. This study confirms their solid participation in policy practice, while simultaneously supporting the need for even greater influence.

REFERENCES

Bent-Goodley, T.B. (2001). Ida B. Wells-Barnett: An uncompromising style. In I.B. Carlton-LaNey (Ed.), *African-American leadership: An empowerment tradition in social welfare history* (pp. 87-98). Washington, DC: NASW Press.

Brown, A.W. and Bailey-Etta, B. (1997). An out of home care system in crisis: Implications for African-American children in the child welfare system. *Child Welfare, 46,* 65-84.

Carlton-LaNey, I.B. (Ed.) (1994). Special issue on the legacy of African-American leadership in social welfare. *Journal of Sociology and Social Welfare, 21,* entire volume.

Carlton-LaNey, I.B. (Ed.) (2001). *African-American leadership: An empowerment tradition in social welfare history.* Washington, DC: NASW Press.

Carlton-LaNey, I.B. and Burwell, N.Y. (Eds.) (1996). *African-American community practice models: Historical and contemporary models.* Binghamton, NY: The Haworth Press, Inc.

Conway, M.M. (1991). *Political participation in the United States.* Washington, DC: Congressional Quarterly Press.

Council on Social Work Education (2001). *Educational Policy and Accreditation Standards.* Alexandria, VA: Author.

Davis, K.E. and Bent-Goodley, T.B. (Eds.) (in press). *The color of social policy.* Alexandria, VA: Council on Social Work Education.

Dear, R.B. and Patti, R.J. (1981). Legislative advocacy: Seven effective tactics. *Social Work, 26,* 289-296.

Domanski, M.D. (1998). Prototypes of social work political participation: An empirical model. *Social Work, 43,* 156-157.

Everett, J.E., Chipungu, S.S., and Leashore, B.R. (Eds.) (1997). *Child welfare: An Africentric perspective.* Rutgers, NJ: Rutgers University Press.

Ezell, M. (1993). The political activity of social workers: A post-Reagan update. *Journal of Sociology and Social Welfare, 20,* 81-97.

Figueira-McDonough, J. (1993). Policy practice: The neglected side of social work intervention. *Social Work, 38,* 179-188.

Fisher, R. (1995). Political social work. *Journal of Social Work Education, 31,* 194-203.

Gibbs, J. and Bankhead, T. (2001). *Preserving privilege: California politics, propositions and people of color.* Westport, CT: Praeger.

Hamilton, D. and Fauri, D. (2001). Social workers' political participation: Strengthening the political confidence of social work students. *Journal of Social Work Education, 37,* 321-332.

Haynes, K.S. and Mickelson, J.S. (2000). *Affecting change: Social workers in the political arena* (Third edition). Boston, MA: Allyn and Bacon.

Hoechstetter, S. (1996). Taking new directions to improve public policy. *Social Work, 41,* 343-346.

Hoechstetter, S. (2001). Key strategist shares thoughts on legislative advocacy. *CSWE Reporter, 49*(1), 40.

Jansson, B.S. (1999). *Becoming an effective policy advocate: From policy practice to social justice* (Third edition). Pacific Grove, CA: Brooks/Cole Publishing.

Jansson, B.S. (2000). Policy analysis. In J. Midgley, M.B. Tracy, and M. Livermore (Eds.), *The handbook of social policy* (pp. 41-52). Thousand Oaks, CA: Sage.

Mahaffey, M. and Hanks, J. (Eds.) (1982). *Practical politics.* Washington, DC: NASW Press.

Powell, J.Y. and Causby, V.D. (1994). From the classroom to the capitol—From MSW students to advocates: Learning by doing. *Journal of Teaching in Social Work, 9*(1/2), 141-154.

Roberts-DeGennaro, M. (1986). Building coalitions for political advocacy. *Social Work, 31,* 308-311.

Rocha, C.J. (2000). Evaluating experiential teaching methods in a policy practice course: The case for service learning to increase political participation. *Journal of Social Work Education, 36,* 53-64.

Salcido, R.M. and Seck, E.T. (1992). Political participation among social work chapters. *Social Work, 37,* 563-565.

Schiele, J.H. (2000). *Human services and the Afrocentric paradigm.* Binghamton, NY: The Haworth Press, Inc.

Schneider, R.L. and Lester, L. (2001). *Social work advocacy: A new framework for action.* Stamford, CT: Brooks/Cole Publishing.

Schneider, R.L. and Netting, F.E. (1999). Influencing social policy in a time of devolution: Upholding social work's great tradition. *Social Work, 44,* 349-357.

Stuart, P.H. (1999). Linking clients and policy: Social worker's distinctive contribution. *Social Work, 44,* 335-348.

Wolk, J.L. (1981). Are social workers politically active? *Social Work, 26,* 283-288.

Wolk, J.L., Pray, J.E., Weismiller, T., and Dempsey, D. (1996). Political practica: Educating social work students for policymaking. *Journal of Social Work Education, 32,* 91-99.

Chapter 2

Implications of Social Security Reform for Wealth Development Among African Americans

Wilhelmina A. Leigh

Although income has long been used to compare the well-being of blacks and whites in this country, only since the mid-1960s (toward the end of the Civil Rights Movement) has wealth been used for this purpose as well. The 1967 Survey of Economic Opportunity—the first government survey that allowed an examination of differences in wealth by race—revealed marked disparities (Terrell, 1971). In 1967 the ratio of black household net worth or wealth ($3,779) to white household net worth or wealth ($20,153) was .188 (18.8 percent). Racial wealth disparities persisted during the remainder of the twentieth century. For example, although net worth for the average black household had risen to $19,736 in 1984 with the comparable figure for white households at $76,297, the ratio of these figures was only .259 (25.9 percent). In 1993, the ratio was virtually unchanged at .26 (26 percent), with mean black household net worth or wealth at $28,416 and mean white household net worth or wealth at $109,132 (Eller and Fraser, 1995; Oliver and Shapiro, 1989; Terrell, 1971).[1] A similar finding emerges with median net worth data from 1995.[2] Median net worth for black households of $7,073 is a fraction (.144 or 14.4 percent) of median net worth for white households of $49,030 (Davern and Fisher, 2001).

Explanations for this persistent gap have included such factors as the intergenerational consequences of the failure in 1863 to provide each emancipated slave the promised forty acres and a mule. Advocacy for a massive capital transfer or reparations has developed around this historical oversight (Browne, 1974; Oliver and Shapiro,

1997).[3] Another posited explanation is the failure of African Americans to invest in the stock market, a shortcoming attributed in part to the lack of familiarity with this market and perceptions of its risk (Brimmer, 1988).

This chapter examines the implications of proposed reforms to maintain the solvency of the Social Security system (based on stock market investment) for wealth development and for bridging the wealth gap between African Americans and whites. The first section discusses patterns of wealth in the African-American community. Next, proposed reforms to the Social Security system are described, along with their likely impacts on African Americans. Finally, the implications for social work practice of these reform proposals are presented.

WEALTH IN THE AFRICAN-AMERICAN COMMUNITY

How is wealth defined? Gross personal wealth is defined as the gross value of all assets (including the full-face value of life insurance, reduced by policy loans), before reduction by the amount of debts. Net personal wealth or net worth is one's level of wealth (or worth) after all debts have been removed from gross personal wealth (Blau and Graham, 1990; Oliver and Shapiro, 1989; U.S. Bureau of the Census, 1990).

In 1967, the $22.7 billion in assets held by blacks constituted 2 percent of the $1,112 billion in total estimated aggregate wealth in the United States (Terrell, 1971). By 1979, blacks reported wealth of $211 billion, nearly ten times their wealth in 1967 but only 4.1 percent of the total wealth at that time of $5,086 billion (O'Hare, 1983).[4] In 1984, African Americans had wealth of $208.2 billion, only 3 percent of the $6,912.2 billion of wealth holdings of all U.S. households that year. Wealth holdings by African Americans as a proportion of all wealth fell short of both their share of money income (7.2 percent) and their share of all households (11 percent) in 1984 (Brimmer, 1988). By 1993, although total U.S. wealth holdings had grown to $9,624.8 billion, the wealth of African Americans ($319.6 billion) remained 3 percent of the total (Eller and Fraser, 1995). African Americans held 7.6 percent of total money income and constituted 11.6 percent of all households at that time. Thus, African Americans continue to have disproportionately small shares of both income and wealth.

Which types of assets constitute wealth? Twelve main types of assets generally are counted as wealth (Eller and Fraser, 1995):

1. Interest-earning assets at financial institutions—passbook savings accounts, money market deposit accounts, certificates of deposit, and interest-earning checking accounts
2. Other interest-earning assets—money market funds, U.S. government securities, municipal and corporate bonds, and other assets
3. Regular checking accounts
4. Stocks and mutual fund shares
5. Equity in business or profession
6. Equity in motor vehicles
7. Equity in own home
8. Rental property equity
9. Other real estate equity
10. U.S. savings bonds
11. IRA or Keogh accounts
12. Other assets—mortgage held from sales of real estate, amount due from the sale of a business, unit trust, and other financial investments

Frequency with Which Assets Are Held

When assets are analyzed by the frequency with which they are held, similar patterns are evident for all asset-holding households. The category for which the largest proportion of households reported holdings in 1995 was equity in motor vehicles, followed by interest-earning assets at financial institutions, and then by equity in own home. Among all U.S. households, 89 percent reported equity in motor vehicles, 69 percent reported interest-earning assets at financial institutions, and 64 percent reported equity in own home. Shares among white households by type of asset are slightly larger—92 percent have motor vehicles, 72 percent have interest-earning assets at financial institutions, and 67 percent have home equity. Shares of black households with these assets are markedly lower—73 percent have equity in motor vehicles, 46 percent have interest-earning assets at financial institutions, and 45 percent have home equity (see Table 2.1).

TABLE 2.1. Assets Held by the Largest Percentages of Households by Race (1995)

	Blacks	Whites	All
Equity in motor vehicles	73	92	89
Interest-earning assets at financial institutions	46	72	69
Equity in own home	45	67	64

Source: Davern and Fisher, 2001

If we examine the only net financial asset among the three most frequently held assets—i.e., interest-earning assets at financial institutions—we find that its dominant form is passbook savings accounts. Passbook savings accounts are held by 60 percent of all asset-holding households, 62 percent of these white households, and 43 percent of these black households (Davern and Fisher, 2001). Other types of net financial assets are held with lesser frequency. In particular, less than a fourth of all households report owning stocks and mutual fund shares—23 percent of white households, but only 6 percent of black households.

Value of Assets

The list of assets with the greatest values differs from the list of most frequently held assets. In addition, differences in the value of asset holdings by race are marked.

Asset values for both the median household and the mean household show a considerable gap between blacks and whites. Net worth for the median asset-holding U.S. household was $37,587 in 1993 (1993 dollars). Among asset-holding white households in 1993, this figure was $45,740, more than ten times the median for asset-holding black households ($4,418). Although the wealth gap between mean black and white households is narrower than the gap between these median households, the mean asset-holding white household has nearly four times ($109,132) the wealth of the mean asset-holding African-American household ($28,416) (see Table 2.2).

TABLE 2.2. Median and Mean Values of Net of Wealth (Net Worth), Asset-Holding Households by Race (1993 and 1995)

	1993 Mean (1993 $)	1993 Median (1993 $)	1995 Mean (1995 $)	1995 Median (1995 $)
Blacks	$ 28,416	$ 4,418	$ 4,653	$ 7,073
Whites	$109,132	$ 45,740	$ 48,177	$ 49,030
All	$ 99,772	$ 37,587	$ 39,590	$ 40,200

Source: Eller and Fraser, 1995 (Unpublished tabulations); Davern and Fisher, 2001

By median asset value, the highest ranking categories of wealth were the same for black and white households in 1993: home equity, rental property equity, other assets, and other real estate equity (see Table 2.3). However, the magnitudes of the asset values differ. By mean asset value, the highest ranking categories of wealth for households in 1993 are: rental property equity, home equity, and equity in business or profession (see Table 2.4). Home equity is the only asset in the top three when assessed both by the frequency with which it is held and by asset value (both median and mean). In 1995, the four top-ranked wealth categories remained the same for white households, although they changed for African-American households (Davern and Fisher, 2001). Equity in own home (62 percent of the median net worth of African-American households in 1995) was the highest-ranked asset for African-American households in both 1993 and 1995. However, in 1995, the asset with the second largest median value was other real estate equity ($18,000), followed by IRA or Keogh accounts ($5,000) and rental property equity and stocks and mutual funds (both valued at $4,000) (see Table 2.5). As might be expected because of the calculation underlying mean values, when these are calculated for 1995 the third of the top three asset categories changes (see Table 2.4). The top categories become rental property equity, equity in one's own home, and other real estate equity (replacing equity in business or profession). Mean values for 1995 are not reported here.

TABLE 2.3. Assets with Largest Median Net Values, Asset-Holding Households by Race (1993)

	Blacks	Whites	All
Equity in own home	$28,800	$49,500	$46,670
Rental property equity	$19,000	$29,300	$29,300
Other assets	NA	$21,860	$21,001
Other real estate equity	$ 8,000	$19,415	$19,415

Source: Eller and Fraser, 1995 (Unpublished tabulations)

Racial disparities persisted after 1995, not only for the median value of home equity ($60,000 for white homeowners versus $29,000 for black homeowners in 1998) but also for the median net wealth reported by owners (*The State of the Nation's Housing,* 2000). White homeowners reported median net wealth in 1998 of $148,920, more than double the $67,280 in median net wealth reported by African-American homeowners.

The median and mean values of net worth in stocks and mutual fund shares are not among the top three assets for households whose heads are either white or black. As with all assets, the median and mean values for holdings of stocks and mutual funds by whites ($7,100 and $40,186, respectively, in 1993, and $9,350 and $41,882, respectively, in 1995) greatly exceed the values for African Americans ($3,900 and $21,543, respectively, in 1993, and $4,000 and $12,305, respectively, in 1995) (see Table 2.6).

Summary and Explanations

Although the rankings of assets by frequency held and value are similar among African-American and white households, the magnitudes of asset values consistently are greater for white households than for black households. The assets owned most frequently by both African-American and white households are motor vehicles, interest-earning assets at financial institutions, and equity in own home. When ranked by their median and mean values, the orderings of assets change completely, however. Only home equity is highly ranked both by frequency (with which the asset is held) and its median and

TABLE 2.4. Assets with Largest Mean Net Values, Asset-Holding Households by Race (1993)

	Blacks	**Whites**	**All**
Rental property equity	$47,707	$78,621	$79,265
Equity in own home	$40,575	$70,802	$68,933
Equity in business or profession	$33,230	$59,856	$59,002

Source: Eller and Fraser, 1995 (Unpublished tabulations)

mean values. Stocks and mutual fund shares are not a major source of investment for African Americans.

How are these patterns explained? Many factors contribute to the observed patterns. To explain these patterns, Blau and Graham (1990) cite the standard model of wealth developed by Modigliani and Brumberg which attributes differences in wealth among families at a given stage in the life cycle to differences in: inherited wealth (or other intergenerational transfers), rates of return on investments, and previous savings. They determined that the difference in inherited wealth or intergenerational transfers is the most likely of the three standard explanations for wealth differences between black and white households. Differences in rates of return on investments were found to account for only a small portion of the black/white wealth gap. Finally, although previous savings depend on differences in lifetime or permanent income, age, and other taste-related sociodemographic factors, Blau and Graham (1990) found no evidence of major racial differences in the propensity to save.

In a more recent analysis of the black/white wealth gap, Altonji, Doraszelski, and Segal (2000) found that blacks would have wealth levels comparable to whites if the relationship between wealth and income and demographics for blacks was the same as it is for whites, and if blacks and whites had the same income and demographic characteristics. They explored the degree to which the black/white wealth gap could be explained by racial differences in any of the following: intervivos transfers and inheritances, savings rates, and rates of return on savings. This analysis found that much of the difference between blacks and whites in the effect of income and demographics on wealth is due to differences in savings behavior and/or in rates of re-

TABLE 2.5. Assets with Largest Median Net Values, Asset-Holding House-holds by Race (1995)

	Blacks	Whites	All
Equity in own home	$31,485	$51,567	$50,000
Rental property equity	$ 4,000	$38,000	$34,250
Other assets	NA	$29,100	$29,100
Other real estate equity	$18,000	$23,000	$22,000

Source: Davern and Fisher, 2001

turn on assets rather than to differences in intervivos transfers and inheritances.

The federal government and the real estate industry are complicit in contributing to the wealth gap, especially as it stems from housing equity (Oliver and Shapiro, 1989; Parcel, 1982). Historical policies and practices have resulted in the reduced likelihood that blacks will own homes and in the likelihood that black-owned homes will have lower market values than white-owned homes (Long and Caudill, 1992). These lower market values clearly influence the amount of inheritable wealth held by black households.

SOCIAL SECURITY REFORM AND AFRICAN-AMERICAN WEALTH

The preceding section has described the patterns of wealth holdings among African-American and white households. Although investments in stocks and mutual fund shares form a small portion (4.7 percent) of the value of wealth reported by African Americans, policy proposals are being discussed to convert the existing Social Security system into a vehicle for accumulating wealth in the stock market (Eller and Fraser, 1995). These proposals are being put forward as a means to shore up a system whose solvency will be strained in the twenty-first century by the mismatch between its pay-as-you-go funding mechanism and the needs generated by demographic changes. Both the nature of the system and likely implications of reform proposals for African Americans are discussed.

TABLE 2.6. Median and Mean Values of Stocks and Mutual Fund Shares, Asset-Holding Households by Race (1993 and 1995)

	Blacks	**Whites**	**All**
Median values			
1993	$ 3,900	$ 7,100	$ 6,960
1995	$ 4,000	$ 9,350	$ 9,000
Mean values			
1993	$21,543	$40,186	$39,888
1995	$12,305	$41,882	$41,214

Source: Eller and Fraser, 1995 (Unpublished tabulations); Davern and Fisher, 2001

Social Security System

Social Security is our nation's social insurance program, which provides monthly benefits to retired and disabled workers, to their families, and to the families of deceased workers. Monthly benefit payments and funds to operate the program come from the Social Security Trust Funds, which are generated by: Social Security (Federal Insurance Contributions Act or FICA) taxes paid by workers (6.2 percent of annual wages up to $84,900 in 2002), and employers (who match their employee's contributions); income taxes that beneficiaries pay on their monthly Social Security payments; and interest earnings on the reserves in the Trust Funds (after obligated payments have been made each year). Social Security reserves (funds left after payments due to annuitants have been made each year) are invested in Treasury bonds, which have low yields. In calendar year 2002, employer and employee FICA taxes accounted for 85 percent of the income to the Social Security Trust Funds, with interest on reserves providing 13 percent and income taxes on benefits 2 percent of this income (Hill and Reno, 2002).

Social Security is a pay-as-you-go system in which the taxes paid by workers and employers in a given year cover the payments that beneficiaries receive that year. For example, in 2002, income of $624 billion was projected for the Trust Funds. Obligations of $465 billion (most of this for benefits, with less than 1 percent for administrative expenses) were anticipated, leaving a surplus of $159 billion to be invested in Treasury bonds (Hill and Reno, 2002). Thus, in the current system, FICA tax revenues are not earmarked for the individuals whose salaries are the base for these taxes.

Social Security is a defined benefit annuity plan—i.e., a formula (rather than investment earnings) determines the amount of monthly Social Security checks. The formula adjusts the level of benefit payments so that persons who formerly were low-wage earners receive a higher percentage of their earnings as their monthly Social Security payments than do persons who formerly were higher-wage earners. (An alternative type of annuity is a defined contribution plan. Annuitized payments from defined contribution plans reflect the amounts paid into an investment vehicle and the yields on these funds.)

As of December 1999, the average monthly Social Security benefit for retired white men receiving benefits based on their work histories was $922.80; for retired black men, it was $756.00 (Social Security Administration, 2000). As of December 1999, the comparable average monthly benefit for retired white women was $706.30, with retired black women receiving $626.80. These patterns in the size of monthly benefit checks reflect differences in the work histories of men and women, disparities in the wages paid to men and women and to blacks and whites for comparable jobs, and different occupational histories by race and gender.

Although black men and black women receive smaller benefit checks on average than their white counterparts, Social Security is the source of retirement income reported by the largest shares of both the white (92 percent) and black (83 percent) elderly (Social Security Administration, 1998). By contrast, asset earnings are reported by two-thirds of the white elderly but only one-third of elderly African Americans. Despite the widespread receipt of Social Security benefits by the black and white elderly and the nearly equal percentages (38 percent for blacks and 41 percent for whites) reporting that Social Security benefits keep them out of poverty, the proportion of elderly African Americans who report being poor even though they receive Social Security payments (24 percent) is triple the comparable share of the white elderly (8 percent) (Social Security Administration, 1999).

In the not-too-distant future, a shortfall is anticipated in the Social Security system because current tax rates (6.2 percent for both employers and employees) are expected to not produce enough revenue to cover the benefit obligations projected over the next seventy-five years. By 2017, tax revenue is expected to be less than outgo for the system. By 2041, both the reserves in the Social Security Trust Funds and interest earnings are expected to be depleted. After this point, the funds coming in annually are expected to meet only 73 percent of benefit costs.[5] This shortfall is driven by the increased longevity among the population, the increased number of retirees due to the aging of the baby boomers (persons born between 1946 and 1964), and the decrease in the number of persons in the workforce paying FICA taxes (relative to the increased number of retirees) (Conrad and Leigh, 1999).

MEETING THE SHORTFALL

There are two general ways to meet the expected Social Security shortfall—reduce benefits, or increase revenue. Benefits could be reduced by: increasing taxes paid by beneficiaries on their monthly payments; freezing annual cost-of-living adjustments to benefit payments; raising the age of eligibility for benefits sooner than the currently scheduled age hikes and increasing it further; reducing benefits for disabled workers and for women who have never worked outside the home; making Social Security means tested; and altering the benefit formula to reduce payments for all future beneficiaries. Of these six proposals, only one (means testing) might prove beneficial to African Americans (Conrad and Leigh, 1999). Because of their lower relative incomes, with means testing, African Americans would be more likely than whites to be eligible for benefits.

Ways to meet the shortfall by increasing revenue include: increasing the payroll tax rate above the current 6.2 percent; expanding coverage to include all workers (especially state and local government employees, one-fourth of whom are not covered); and allowing the federal government or individuals who pay FICA taxes to invest a portion of these funds in the stock market (generally referred to as privatization). This last method to increase revenue has clear implications for wealth development.

Privatization and Wealth Development

When first discussed during the mid-1990s, privatization was considered in two forms, one with the federal government investing all the Social Security assets (as a single account) in stocks or mutual fund shares and the other with each covered worker having a separate investment account. More recently, the debate has centered around plans with individual investment accounts.

All privatization proposals involve converting the existing pay-as-you-go system into a prefunded system. In a prefunded system, payments made by individuals would be retained and invested on their behalf. Thus, in any given year, FICA tax deductions would be applied toward the future benefits of a given worker, rather than to pay benefits for currently retired individuals.

Because current retirees (who worked and paid into the pay-as-you-go system) would still be owed payments and would not have individual accounts with privately invested assets, meeting payment obligations to current retirees while simultaneously privatizing the Social Security system would involve sizable transition costs. As much as $8.9 trillion over the first several decades under a privatized system could be required to pay benefits to current and near-future retirees on the basis of their past Social Security contributions (Orszag and Orszag, 2000). Some of this cost will be for administrative expenses to establish and manage the roughly 150 million individual investment accounts.

A privatized Social Security system would no longer be a defined benefit plan. Instead, Social Security would be a defined contribution plan, under which annuity amounts would depend on the following: how much was paid into the account, how the funds were invested, and when the withdrawal of proceeds from the investment account begins. As the basis for the social insurance system of the United States, a defined contribution plan would entail risks. Additional expenditures would be required to support during retirement those persons who invest unwisely or who must cash out their investments when sales prices are low relative to purchase prices.

To enable Social Security account holders to invest wisely under a privatized system, money also will need to be spent to educate all citizens about investment options and strategies. As the 1990s and the first years of the twenty-first century have reminded all of us, stock market yields at any moment are subject to change. Thus, investors may wind up buying high and selling low, rather than the preferred modus operandi of buying low and selling high. Also, the movement of large sums of money into stocks and mutual funds at one time, which privatization of the Social Security system would entail, virtually guarantees that stock market returns will drop; this sizable cash infusion would increase the supply of money in the stock market so much that the price of money (or market yields) would fall.

Although it is straightforward to specify the categories of expenses anticipated due to privatization, much of the debate and discussion has centered around the anticipated timing, the amount of expenditures, and how to provide funds to cover them. Impacts on African Americans (and other largely low-income populations) show up when comparisons are made between projected future benefit payments from a privatized Social Security system and from the system either not shored up or shored up without privatization. The question thus becomes whether any proposal guarantees African Americans more monthly income than the 73 percent of today's benefit schedule that is the projected payout level under the insolvent Social Security system between 2041 and 2076 (Hill and Reno, 2002).

Since the stock market offers guarantees to no one—its yields increase with the riskiness of the investments—the comfort level of African Americans with stock market investment becomes a key determinant of the likely impact on their wealth of Social Security reform proposals involving privatization. To date, African Americans have invested little in stocks and mutual fund shares, less than 5 percent of all their assets and with slightly more than 5 percent of the population reporting holding these assets. Thus, the need for education and guidance targeted to African Americans to ease them into stock market investment under a reformed Social Security system might be greater than for the population at large (Brimmer, 1988; Eller and Fraser, 1995).

IMPLICATIONS FOR SOCIAL WORK PRACTICE

Having explored the retrofitting of the Social Security system to become a vehicle for individual wealth accumulation, let us now go back to the list of assets defined as wealth and see what social workers could do to help foster general wealth development for African Americans.[6] Consider the assets in which either a sizable percentage of African Americans already have holdings or for which the median/mean value of the asset is sizable—e.g., motor vehicles, home equity, real property equity, other real estate equity, interest-earning assets at financial institutions, and other assets. How can African-American social workers influence the holdings of these assets by African Americans?

Micro-Level Intervention

At a micro level, the role for African-American social workers would be to make sure their clients received the best deals or prices possible when acquiring these assets. Social workers could play the ombudsman role by assembling relevant information about the most common investments and making the information available to their clients. The education and information social workers can provide could begin with basic instruction about money management and could extend to knowledge about where to refer clients.

Investment Planning

Other assets could perhaps be tapped into more by African Americans. Investments in the category other interest-earning assets (including money market funds, municipal and corporate bonds, and U.S. government securities) are reported by 9 percent of white households but only 1 percent of households that are African-American. Equity in business or profession is reported by 11 percent of white households, but only 3 percent of African-American households. U.S. savings bonds are held by 20 percent of white households but only 9 percent of black households. IRA and Keogh accounts are held by a slightly higher percentage of white households (27 percent) than are stocks and mutual fund shares (23 percent), although these investments are held by 8 percent and 5 percent of African-American households respectively (Davern and Fisher, 2001). A similar educational/informational approach could be taken with respect to investment in these assets, although it probably would require more effort on the part of social workers to stimulate investment in or acquisition of these less commonly held assets among their clientele with disposable income.

Referrals

A critical role that African-American social workers could play would be to refer their clients to places where they could learn more about the many forms of wealth and assets they could acquire. For example, to increase the home equity of their clients, social workers could make referrals to housing counseling centers, local chapters of Habitat for Humanity, HUD Locator Centers/Community Builders, or the Wall Street project (Firms Start Homeowner Drive, 2000). Alternatively, to enhance their holdings of interest-bearing assets at financial institutions, social workers could refer clients to financial institutions known to be making outreach to underserved populations and areas.

Lower-Income Clients

For lower-income clients, in the context of TANF (Temporary Assistance for Needy Families) and SSI (Supplemental Security Income), African-American social workers could provide guidance to individuals who set up an IDA (Individual Development Account) about wise uses for these funds (Corporation for Enterprise Development, 2000; Sherraden and Sherraden, 2000). Also in the context of TANF, African-American social workers could provide information about and assistance to enable beneficiaries to tap into TANF dollars to get training and support for the development of microenterprises (Greenberg, 1999). Many of the referrals that can be made will be specific to the jurisdictions in which the social workers are employed and to institutions located there.

Influencing Policy

Although social workers are most commonly known for serving individual clients, they also can play a role in influencing policy both locally and nationally. To be able to do this effectively, social workers would need to stay abreast of national, state, and local issues related to a wide range of topics. Although having time to do this becomes a challenge, the following suggestions may help:

1. To facilitate self-education (about policy issues), African-American social workers could join topical (e.g., homeownership, welfare reform) local interest groups.
2. African-American social workers could link with numerous sources of information by signing up for topical Listservs on the Internet.
3. A Listserv targeted to African-American social workers also could provide a means to share relevant information about policy needs and initiatives. The Listserv mechanism could be a springboard for greater activism, as well, if African-American

social workers use it to organize campaigns to support/oppose legislative initiatives.

4. An annual policy conference could expose African-American social workers to a range of issues and make them aware of organizations and individuals with whom they should/could become involved to keep current between conferences.

5. African-American social workers could add their names to the mailing lists for the departments of local, state, and federal governments most germane to their clients' needs, as a way to stay abreast of changes in regulations or public meetings at which the input of their clients or themselves might influence the policy process.

CONCLUSION

African-American social workers often are in contact with those in need of a range of services and who could benefit from knowledge about many topics. Providing services and moving clients beyond their need for services (which wealth development could do) becomes one of the challenges for African-American social workers. Yet another challenge for social workers is remaining current with the broader policies that influence the fields in which they work. Existing technology can assist with this, but social workers, along with other professionals, may find that the time to access, synthesize, and use the information acquired becomes the next challenge. This chapter offers selected ideas that could help social workers meet this challenge in the area of wealth development.

NOTES

1. Wealth is reported only for those households that reported any asset holdings. Therefore households with no reported assets are excluded from these comparisons.

2. Median net worth is the value that divides asset-holding households into two equal size groups—those whose net worth exceeds this amount and those whose net worth falls short of it.

3. To redress this failure of government policy, several prominent African Americans—including Randall Robinson of Transafrica and Representative John Conyers—have advocated for the payment of reparations to the descendants of slaves in America.

4. The percentages for 1967 and 1979 are computed with black wealth as the percentage of the sum of black wealth and white wealth, excluding the holdings of the then very small non-black minority population.

5. Current projections are that FICA tax revenues will meet 73 percent of the obligations of the Social Security program between 2041 and 2076, but only 66 percent thereafter. See Hill and Reno (2002) for further information.

6. It is assumed herein that African-American social workers are more likely than social workers of other races/ethnicities to serve African-American clientele. Suggestions could be implemented by social workers of any race/ethnicity with their appropriately low-income clients of any race/ethnicity, however.

REFERENCES

Altonji, J.G., Doraszelski, U., and Segal, L. (2000). Black/white differences in wealth. *Economic Perspectives (Federal Reserve Bank of Chicago), 24,* 38-50.

Blau, F.D. and Graham, J.W. (1990). Black-white differences in wealth and asset composition. *Quarterly Journal of Economics, 105,* 321-339.

Brimmer, A.F. (1988). Income, wealth, and investment behavior in the black community. *The American Economic Review (Papers and Proceedings), 78,* 151-155.

Browne, R.S. (1974). Wealth distribution and its impact on minorities. *The Review of Black Political Economy, 4,* 27-37.

Conrad, C.A. and Leigh, W.A. (1999). *Social Security reform: What proposed changes mean for African Americans (An issue brief).* Washington, DC: Joint Center for Political and Economic Studies.

Corporation for Enterprise Development (2000). *Individual development accounts: A tool for building savings and wealth for working-poor Americans (A fact sheet).* Washington, DC: Author.

Davern, M.E. and Fisher, P.J. (2001). *Household net worth and asset ownership: 1995.* U.S. Bureau of the Census and U.S. Government Printing Office. Current Population Reports, P70-71.

Eller, T.J. and Fraser, W. (1995). *Asset ownership of households: 1993.* Washington, DC: U.S. Bureau of the Census and U.S. Government Printing Office. Current Population Reports, P70-47. Unpublished tabulations of raw data on which this report was based, accessed at World Wide Web page <http://www.census.gov/prod/1/pop/p70-47.pdf> on March 24, 2000 and March 28, 2000.

Firms Start Homeowner Drive. (2000). *Housing affairs letter,* No. 00-16, 3.

Greenberg, M. (1999). *Developing policies to support microenterprise in the TANF structure: A guide to the law.* Washington, DC: Microenterprise Fund for Innovation, Effectiveness, Learning and Dissemination (FIELD) of the Aspen Institute.

Hill, C. and Reno, V. (2002). *Social Security finances: Findings of the 2002 Trustees Report (Social Security brief).* Washington, DC: National Academy of Social Insurance.

Long, J.E. and Caudill, S.B. (1992). Racial differences in homeownership and housing wealth, 1970-1986. *Economic Inquiry, 30,* 83-100.

O'Hare, W.P. (1983). *Wealth and economic status: A perspective on racial inequity.* Washington, DC: Joint Center for Political Studies.

Oliver, M.L. and Shapiro, T.M. (1989). Race and wealth. *The Review of Black Political Economy, 17,* 5-25.

Oliver, M.L. and Shapiro, T.M. (1997). *Black wealth/white wealth: A new perspective on racial inequality.* New York and London: Routledge.

Orszag, P.R. and Orszag, J.M. (2000). *All that glitters is not gold: The Feldstein-Liebman analysis of reforming Social Security with individual accounts.* Washington, DC: Center on Budget and Policy Priorities.

Parcel, T.L. (1982). Wealth accumulation of black and white men: The case of housing equity. *Social Problems, 30,* 199-211.

Sherraden, M.I. and Sherraden, M.A. (2000). Asset building: Integrating research, education and practice. *Advances in Social Work, 1,* 61-77.

Social Security Administration (1998). *Income of the aged chartbook, 1996.* SSA Publication No. 13-11727. Washington, DC: Author.

Social Security Administration (1999). *Fast facts and figures about Social Security.* SSA Publication No. 13-11785.

Social Security Administration (2000). *Annual statistical supplement, 2000.* World Wide Web page <http://www.ssa.gov/statistics/Supplement/2000/> (last modified May 12, 2000).

Terrell, H.S. (1971). Wealth accumulation of black and white families: The empirical evidence. *The Journal of Finance, 26,* 363-377.

Chapter 3

African-American Grandparent Caregivers: Eliminating Double Jeopardy in Social Policy

Sandra Edmonds Crewe

> Grandparents . . . perform an extraordinary service which pre-
> vents hundreds of thousands of children from coming to the at-
> tention of the public child protection system. . . . The costs
> savings in both human and fiscal terms are enormous. (Genera-
> tions United, 1999, pp. 15-16)

African-American elders have historically cared for their grandchildren and other kin. Their caring for their grandchildren is a part of
a kinship care tradition that is unique and reflects "complex cultural,
environmental, and institutional factors that define Black family life
in America" (Brown and Mars, 2000, p. 203). Today African-American grandparents are more likely to be primary caregivers for their
grandchildren than any other group of caregivers. This legacy of kinship care is a source of both pain and pride (Burlingame, 1999) that
dates back to the cultural traditions of the tribes of West Africa
(Fuller-Thomson and Minkler, 2000; Smith, 2000). Most (56 percent) African-American children live with one or both of their parents, however, over 50 percent of those who do not live with parent(s)
live with grandparents (Smith, 2000). Through formal and informal
arrangements, African-American grandparents make a tremendous
contribution to their families and society as a whole. Yet, they are un-
sung heroes who often face this added responsibility without social

policy that responds to their needs for instrumental and emotional support.

A growing body of literature on grandparents as primary caregivers of grandchildren documents the savings to the public welfare system. In many states, California as an exemplar, it ultimately costs less to have grandparents as caregivers than it is to have children placed in nonrelative foster care (Dornin, 1996). Despite the cost benefits to the public welfare system, it generally fails to favorably acknowledge the millions of dollars relative caregivers save through self-sacrifice. Likewise, public policy fails to effectively address the documented caregiver stress and other adverse effects on grandparents' well-being. Grandparents' sense of family responsibility is preyed upon by enacting policies and practices that exploit their strengths and resiliency. Brown and Mars (2000) assert that grandparent caregiver families should be applauded for the positive aspects of their surrogate parenting. However, they urge "social scientists, social policymakers and practitioners to remain vigilant regarding circumstances of stress and strain, particularly in low-income families where surrogate parenting may not be conducive to the well-being of the child or the grandparent caregiver" (p. 215).

This chapter examines the critical role of African-American grandparent caregivers and advocates for more "grandparent-friendly" policies that reward rather than penalize them for their contributions. Using double jeopardy as a framework, this chapter examines the unique experiences of older African Americans raising grandchildren. The chapter also discusses and acknowledges the need for African-American organizations to take a leading role in promulgating public policy that uses the 2000 census data on caregiving to address the systemic lack of support to older African Americans who are raising grandchildren.

GUARDIANS OF GENERATIONS:
AFRICAN-AMERICAN GRANDPARENTS

African-American grandmothers have an esteemed role in the African-American community. In his seminal work, *The Negro Family in the United States,* E. Franklin Frazier (1939) described black grandmothers as *guardians of generations*. The arts and media contribute to this image. Movies such as *Soul Food* acknowledge the powerful role of the grandmother in an extended family. Similarly, professional athletes such as Shannon and Sterling Sharpe add to the positive image by publicly acknowledging and honoring their grandmother on network television for raising them. Maya Angelou's poem, "Our Grandmothers," is yet another positive portrayal of the strength and resiliency of grandmothers (Angelou, 1994; Burton and Devries, 1992). Similarly, social science literature cites the dynamic contributions of African-American grandmothers through discussions about the extended family, kinship care, surrogate parenting, and intergenerational families (Fuller-Thomson and Minkler, 2000; Feldman, 1997; Gibson, 1999; Roe and Minkler, 1999). The image of the elder grandmother as the strong matriarch of the African-American family has been both a source of pride and controversy in literature. Although her contributions to the stability and transmission of culture in the African-American community is widely acknowledged and celebrated as a strength, inadequate attention has been given to the public policy response to the added burdens of parenting "again and again." Casper and Bryson (1998) report about two-thirds of grandchildren in homes maintained by a grandmother and no spouse are in poverty.

Although the literature is rich with references to the role of African-American grandmothers, less is written about the grandfather's role in the family and public welfare system. Lempert (1999) explains "contemporary social imagery of the absent African American fathers links 'African American families' and 'matriarchy' so successfully that the terms have become both synonymous and ubiquitous" (p. 190). Social science literature and research has followed suit by overlooking the role of grandfathers as caregivers and justifying it by citing their low numbers. This in itself reinforces a negative image. Their low level of participating in research may well reflect both individual and societal social construction of caregiving as "gendered" work (McAdoo, 1993). Yet, the anecdotal evidence and a growing number of qualitative studies are documenting that grandfathers have also carried much of the burden of the welfare system. Burton and Devries (1992) describe the feelings of a sixty-two-year-old grandfather who is a caregiver:

I got a lot on my back. I take care of my wife who has cancer and my two grandbabies. Sometimes, I think it's a losing battle. But

> I have faith in the Almighty and I have two good boys who help me. They aren't able to be here all the time because they have families too. You can't ask for more than that. (p. 4)

Lempert's research showed that African-American grandfathers often work in concert with their spouses in assuming primary care responsibilities as well as serving as financial providers, decision makers, and protectors of the family. However, grandfather caregivers are marginalized by rules of quantitative research that disregard them because of their "lack of statistical presence." This lack of focus is likely to change because during the 1990s, grandfather only, neither parent present, had the greatest growth (39 percent) in grandparent maintained households (Casper and Bryson, 1998). In the 2000 census, grandfathers represent almost 38 percent of grandparents caring for their grandchildren (Grandsplace; U.S. Census Bureau: Table PCT014).

Social science literature often reduces family types to male, female, and dual-headed households. Grandparent households are sometimes grouped in the following five types: (1) both grandparents, some parents present; (2) both grandparents, no parents present; (3) grandmother only, some parents present; (4) grandmother only, no parents present; and (5) grandfather only (Casper and Bryson, 1998). Smith (2000) reports that although the analysis of the literature suggests that the concept of kinship care exists on a continuum related to formality of the care, the research usually focuses on the ends of the continuum and neglects any middle of the continuum variations that might exist. This is an inadequate approach to use in analyzing the African-American family caregiver structure because of its numerous variations. Billingsley (1968) developed a typology that highlighted the structural diversity of African-American families by presenting a typology of thirty-two kinds of family structures. Thus grandmother and grandfather maintained caregiver households are simplifications of much more complex family structures. Hill (1997) uses the concept of flexible family roles to further explicate the variations within African-American families.

An ecological perspective helps to better understand the pressures placed on African-American grandparents to assume parental responsibility for grandchildren. The macro system that represents the attitudes and ideologies of the culture is particularly strong as it relates to elevating family responsibility in the African-American community. The environment contributes to low-income grandparents minimizing stresses out of fear that their grandchildren will be removed from their homes (Robertson, 1997) and that they would break the highly valued family tradition of caring for their own. In addition, they focus on the rewards and downplay health limitations (Burton, 1992; Minkler, Rose, and Price, 1992). This is most likely tied to fusion of faith and family responsibility within the African-American community.

GRANDPARENT CAREGIVERS— EMERGING PUBLIC POLICY

Throughout the 1990s, public policies were enacted to respond to the growing trend of grandparents rearing grandchildren. President Clinton signed a formal proclamation declaring 1995 as the Year of the Grandparent (Administration on Aging [AoA], 1997). In addition, the 1995 White House Conference on Aging passed two resolutions supporting increased assistance to older relatives raising grandchildren and the U.S. Congress mandated in the 1996 welfare reform law that the 2000 census collect data on grandparent caregiving (AoA, 1997; Bryson, 2001; Minkler, 2001). In 1996, the president also proclaimed Thanksgiving week as "National Family Caregivers Week." These initiatives were driven by a response to a congressional hearing in 1992 that focused national attention on the parenting roles being assumed by grandparents and increased the public awareness of intergenerational caregiving. The urgency was confirmed by the 1997 census data that showed nearly five million grandparents were serving as caregivers for their grandchildren (Casper and Bryson, 1998). The AoA acknowledged the need for special funding, and included the National Family Caregiver Support Program (NFCSP) in the Older Americans Act (OAA) Amendments of 2000 (PL 106-501). AoA set aside 10 percent of its total funds to support the needs of over sixty-year-old relative caregivers and their children (AoA, n.d.).

The NFCSP was developed by the AoA to form partnerships with area offices on aging and local community service providers to support family caregivers by providing the following:

- Information to caregivers about available services
- Assistance to caregivers in gaining access to supportive services

- Individual counseling, organization of support groups, and caregiver training to assist the caregivers in making decisions and solving problems relating to caregiving roles
- Respite care to enable caregivers to be temporarily relieved from their caregiving responsibilities; and supplemental services, on a limited basis, to complement that care provided by caregivers

The NFCSP serves both family caregivers of older adults and grandparents and relative caregivers of children not more than eighteen years of age, including grandparents who are sole caregivers of grandchildren and those individuals who are affected by mental illness or who have developmental disabilities (AoA, n.d.) This is a landmark policy in aging in that it includes grandchildren as eligible recipients of benefits, thus paving the way for more intergenerational programs in other previously age restricted areas.

The grandparent caregivers 2000 census data show 6.3 percent of U.S. children (4.5 million) under eighteen years are living in grandparent headed households, a third (1.5 million) of whom have no parent present (Bryson, 2001). In addition, these data show that almost 19 percent of the 2.35 million primary caregiver grandparents had incomes below the poverty level, 35 percent had been caregivers for five or more years, and almost 56 percent are still in the workforce. Table 3.1 gives more findings from the 2000 census related to grandparent caregivers.

These data are likely to support and continue the policy momentum of the decade of the 1990s through the current decade and invite more grandparent caregiver specific policies and practices. Organizations are already including specific grandparent caregiver recommendations. For example, NASW (2001) provides a policy statement that advocates "support programs that enable grandparents to become formal or informal caregivers to grandchildren including particularly financial support" (p. 285). Also, in their legislative agenda for the 107th Congress, Generations United (2001) has recommended legislation to support new housing policies, including a fair housing initiative to fund a "grandfamily" program.

TABLE 3.1. Selected Figures on Grandparents Raising Grandchildren from Census 2000

	Number	Percentage
Grandparents responsible for own grandchildren under 18	2,350,477	
Grandmothers	1,461,062	62.2
Grandfathers	889,415	37.8
Married grandparents	1,717,620	73.1
Grandparents in workforce	1,313,455	55.8
Income below poverty level	441,850	18.7
Care of children for less than one year	573,965	24.4
Care of children for 1-2 years	561,256	23.8
Care of children for 3-4 years	412,676	17.5
Care of children for 5 or more years	839,580	35.7

Source: U.S. Census Bureau (n.d.a, n.d.b)

THE INCREASE IN GRANDPARENT CAREGIVERS: A COMBINATION OF INDIVIDUAL AND SYSTEMIC FACTORS

According to a U.S. Bureau of the Census report on grandparent maintained households between 1970 and 1997, there was a 76 percent increase in grandparents rearing grandchildren (Casper and Bryson, 1998). Between 1990 and 1997 the increase was 19 percent. Of the 4 million grandparent-maintained households reported in 1997, the majority of the grandparents were younger than age 65, 48 percent are between 50 and 64, and 19 percent are 65 and older. The median age of grandparent caregivers is 59.3 years with over half being 60 years and above (Minkler, 2001). Researchers have reported that grandparent caregivers are 60 percent more likely to live in poverty than grandparents who are not raising grandchildren.

Literature documents a myriad of reasons that grandparents find themselves in caregiving roles. Reasons include parental illness and death, emotional problems, substance abuse, out-of-wedlock births, teen pregnancy, homicide, parental incarceration, economic crises, child abuse and neglect, and other family circumstances that render the biological parent unable or unwilling to care for their children (American Association of Retired Persons, 2001; Brown and Mars, 2000; Casper and Bryson, 1998; Fuller-Thomson and Minkler, 2000; Kivnick and Sinclair, 1996; Roe and Minkler, 1998/1999; Smith and Beltran, 2000; Whitley, Kelley, and Sipe, 2001). Although all of these circumstances contribute to the placement of children with grandparents, some are more important than others. Whitley, Kelley, and Sipe (2001) document substance abuse as the leading cause grandparents assume custodial care of grandchildren and the addiction of parents contributes to abandonment, neglect, and abuse.

Changes in social forces also have contributed to the rise in grandparents rearing grandchildren. Smith and Beltran (2000) identify divorce, poverty, high rates of incarceration resulting from harsher drug laws and mandatory sentencing, unemployment, and lack of available foster care homes as important variables that contribute to the higher numbers of grandparents caring for grandchildren. In fact, they report that kinship policy preferences that have been established by many child welfare agencies have resulted in grandparent and other relative placements surpassing traditional foster care. Fuller-Thomson and Minkler (2000) trace the growth to federal, state, and local policies beginning in 1979 that "had the effect of encouraging and requiring that a preference be given to next of kin in the placement of foster children" (p. 2). These changes explain increases in formal placements; however, they do not adequately explain the corresponding rise in informal placements with grandparents in the 1990s (Fuller-Thomson and Minkler, 2000).

Grandparent "caregivers are being confronted with the fallout from the reform of the nation's welfare system" (Hushbeck, n.d., p. 1). The implementation of the 1996 Personal Responsibility and Work Opportunity Reconciliation Act (PRWORA) (PL 104-191) is one possible explanation of the increased informal placements with grandparents. Mandatory work requirements may force some recipients to place children with their parents rather than risk full family sanctions for failing to comply with requirements. Keigher and Fendt

(1998) state that "the nation's rush to make poor mothers 'work or else' is extracting a high price from children, disadvantaged people, people with disabilities, caregivers, and mothers" (p. 229). There has been an increase in the percentage of child-only cases and many of these children are with grandparents. In 1999, there were 770,000 child-only cases which accounted for 29 percent of the TANF caseload (USDHHS, 2001). This represented an increase in both numbers and the proportion of children since 1998. Nationwide, 22 percent of these children are being cared for by grandparents (USDHHS, 2000: Table 26.1-FY 99) providing evidence that grandparents raising grandchildren have been affected by the welfare reform law (Hushbeck, n.d.). Some states, including South Dakota, West Virginia, Hawaii, Indiana, and Idaho have rates ranging from 50 to 73 percent of grandparents raising grandchildren. This means that these grandparents receive cash assistance solely for their grandchildren. Many are also likely not to receive food stamps due to eligibility rules that consider the total household income. For grandparents who receive the TANF grant, the work requirement remains. Grandparents are not exempted from this work requirement. Thus the safety net that they provide for some of the nation's most vulnerable children can sometimes be eroded by a mandatory work requirement.

Increased informal and formal placements are also likely to be related to inadequacies in the support system for low-income families. Lengthy waiting lists for affordable housing, lack of available treatment for substance abuse, and a lack of special needs and transitional housing may also add to the reliance on grandparents to care for grandchildren. Also, many African-American grandparents avoid the red tape and scrutiny they feel is associated with formal arrangements with the child welfare and public assistance systems. Some have commented that the instrumental assistance is not commensurate with the physical and emotional effort to receive the benefits.

DOUBLE JEOPARDY

Grandparents United for Children cite that the majority (68 percent) of grandparent caregivers are white (n.d.). However, middle-aged and older African Americans are twice as likely to be grandparent caregivers as whites in the same age groups (Grandparents

United for Children, n.d.). According to Casper and Bryson (1998) comparatively, in the mid-1990s, 13.5 percent of African-American children lived with grandparents or other relatives compared with 6.5 percent of Hispanic children and 4.1 percent of white children. Correspondingly, they report that 30 percent of African-American grandmothers and 14 percent of African-American grandfathers reported having cared for a grandchild for at least six months. These data are compared with 10.9 percent of all grandparents, thus highlighting the racial disparities. Other studies have also confirmed the disparities in caregiving based on race. Bengston's 1985 cross-cultural study as cited by Kivnick and Sinclair (1996) reported that 60 percent of blacks over sixty years old report having raised fictive kin and grandchildren as compared to only 8 percent among whites.

These findings are consistent with early literature on aging policy that documents the historical differential experiences of African Americans because of the combined effects of race and age. In 1964, the National Urban League (NUL) released a study, *Double Jeopardy,* and explained that,

> Today's aged Negro is different from today's aged White because he *is* Negro . . . and this alone should be enough basis for differential treatment. For he has, indeed, been placed in double jeopardy: first, by being Negro and second by being aged. Age merely compounded the hardships accrued to him as a result of being a Negro. (1964, p. i)

Tally and Kaplan are credited with first raising the double jeopardy hypothesis in 1956 relative to the unequal status of African Americans (Hooyman and Kiyak, 2002). Sometimes it is referred to as the double burden on people of color (Greene, 2000) and is often manifested by health disparities. When the focus is on African-American women, *triple jeopardy* is used to transmit the confounding of three sets of barriers and stereotypes (Mbanaso, Brown, and Ukawuilulu, 2002). Today the double jeopardy hypothesis has been expanded to other people of color and states "that aging persons of color are in jeopardy in our society due to both growing old and being part of an ethnic minority" (Hooyman and Kiyak, 2002, p. 457). The following discussion on African-American caregivers is grounded in the double jeopardy hypothesis because of its value in using a life course perspective in understanding the unique culture and history of African

Americans and its importance in crafting policy to address their needs. Double jeopardy is particularly important in policy analysis. It suggests that the "two disadvantages of race and age combine in ways that make 'the whole greater than the sum of its parts' and implies that programs and policies that simply equalize resources cannot remove accumulated disadvantage" (Pampel, 1998, p. 81). Thus, to overcome cumulative disadvantage, social policies must do more than address equal access.

Current research continues to find that race matters in the well-being of custodial grandparents. Brown and Mars (2000) state that surrogate parenting for African Americans is different from their white counterparts because of the confluence of cultural differences and sociodemographic circumstances that result in fewer economic resources, lower levels of education, marital status, living arrangements, (larger) multiple generation households, and social stresses associated with lifelong poverty. This is particularly true of many grandparents who often have to stretch already inadequate social security benefits to meet basic household needs such as food and clothing. These grandparents are more likely to have to bear both the social and financial burden of child care and thus deplete the already inadequate resources available to meet their newly configured household needs. This economic strain, according to Porterfield, Dressel, and Barnhill (2000, p. 109) "ranges from the elimination of discretionary spending to not being able to afford such necessities as food." Although most willingly take on this added responsibility, which they feel is rightly theirs, they often express resentment of the "endless red tape to acquire meager benefits" (Porterfield, Dressel, and Barnhill, 2000, p. 190). Burdened by the system, these families "make do."

Box 3.1 provides further evidence of the cumulative effect of disparities on African-American elders. Flaherty, Facteau, and Garver (1999) caution that the ease with which it appears that African-American grandmothers assume primary caregiver roles may disguise the acceptability of the arrangement.

Being a part of a culture that places this role on a pedestal possibly results in added pressure and stress to assume this role of parenting again. Although grandmother caregivers show high rates of depression, rate their health as poor, and suffer with frequent multiple chronic health problems, many report positive benefits from their caregiver roll (Burton and Devries, 1992; Roe and Minkler, 1999).

BOX 3.1. Indicators of Double Jeopardy

- African-American life expectancy is 70.2 years compared to an average of 76.5 years for all population groups. This difference is even more striking among African-American men, who have a life expectancy of 66.1 years compared to the national average of 73.6 years for all men.
- More than 68 percent of African-American elders are poor, marginally poor, or economically vulnerable. African-American elders are more than one and a half times as likely as white elders to live below the poverty line. More than one in four African-American elders have incomes that fall below the poverty line.
- More than 10 percent of the nation's 22.4 million caregiving households are African American. More than half of African-American caregivers find themselves sandwiched between caring for an older person and caring for a younger person.
- African-American caregivers are more likely to live with the care recipient and spend an average of 20.6 hours per week providing care. In addition, 66 percent of African-American caregivers are employed full- or part-time.
- Nearly 40 percent of African-American women ages 65 and older live alone compared to 19 percent of African-American males aged 65 years and older. African-American elders are less likely to be married than white elders.

Source: Serving Our African American Elders, U.S. Administration on Aging, <http://www.aoa.gov>

A study of 100 African-American grandmothers rearing their grandchildren found that their physical functioning had the potential of jeopardizing both their health and their grandchildren's health (Whitley, Kelley, and Sipe, 2001). Fuller-Thomson and Minkler (2001) found that "African American caregivers were significantly more likely than non caregiving peers to have limitations in their five activities of daily living" (p. 5). Equally important is the finding that they had more depression symptoms when compared with non-caregiving peers. Clinical depression was observed in one-third of caregivers as compared to only one-fifth of non-caregivers. These findings help to more fully appreciate the continued double jeopardy faced by aging African-American caregivers. Burton and Devries (1992) present this as a policy question: "Will we as a society create support for grandparents so they can survive the challenges?" The answer requires an examination and subsequent assessment of practices and policies that pose obstacles to grandparents raising grandchildren.

PREDATORY PRACTICES AND POLICY RECOMMENDATIONS

The willingness of African-American grandparents to care for their grandchildren makes them vulnerable to policies that are in some ways predatory because they take advantage of their strong family ties and sense of family responsibility. Numerous policies affect the caregivers' financial well-being as well as their ability to do what is best to promote the overall well-being of their grandchildren, including guardianship, the food stamp program, housing, and welfare reform.

Guardianship Rules

Grandparents who care for grandchildren often find themselves in situations in which they cannot properly meet the needs of their grandchildren because of rules that require guardianship. For example, children cannot be enrolled in school or receive medical care because of lack of proper consents. Often the grandparents are not willing to take legal actions to obtain guardianship because they feel it will cause even more strain with the parents. Others avoid the options of guardianship because they remain hopeful that the parents will "get their act together" and resume the caregiver responsibility. Without the required guardianship, they are denied needed assistance for the children.

Alternatives to current guardianship rules are needed. Smith and Beltran (2000) have suggested subsidized guardianships and consent laws that will allow grandparents to enroll children in school and obtain needed medical care.

Food Stamp Program

When grandparents voluntarily assume the care of children, they are not automatically entitled to food stamps. Food stamps guidelines require that the total household income be considered for reasons of eligibility. Thus, their Social Security and other retirement earnings make them ineligible. Although they may have been struggling to make ends meet without the added responsibilities of grandchildren, the financial strain is even greater when new members are added to the household. There is no justification for this policy considering the reported underutilization of the food stamp program (GAO, 2000, 2001).

A policy recommendation is to uncouple food stamp eligibility from household income and make custodial grandparents automatically eligible for food stamps based upon the number of children they care for. Another option is to raise the income ceilings to make more grandparent caregivers eligible.

Housing

Many grandparents are forced to alter their housing because of space and public policy. Some research has indicated a high level of transience among caregiver grandparents (Flaherty, Facteau, and Garver, 1999). When children are placed in the custodial care of grandparents, housing standards are often lowered to accommodate the placement. Although this facilitates the placement, it fails to recognize the full impact on the household. Other housing issues arise when grandparents reside in assisted housing for elderly families that prohibit children because of the special nature of the housing. Grandparents are required to have custody before being able to add children to a lease and transfer to a larger unit. Receiving custody is sometimes difficult due to the instability or unwillingness of parents. Thus grandparents may be forced to give up their subsidized housing to care for grandchildren. As a result of the dilemma, some grandparents face eviction because they house the grandchildren in violation of their leases. Others are forced to provide housing in a clandestine manner to avoid lease violations. Also, housing children under the "child only" provision of TANF can result in increased rent based upon the TANF grant. Thus, a part of the minimal assistance given to support the children is used to pay increased rent.

Several policy recommendations address these problems. First, public housing authorities and Section Eight administrators should be lobbied to add a preference for grandparent caregivers. The Quality Housing and Work Responsibility Act (PL 105-276) allows local housing agencies flexibility to establish grandfamily preferences. Also, models such as the Grandfamilies House in Massachusetts should be expanded nationwide (Minkler, 2001; Takas, 2001; Smith and Beltran, 2000). Grandfamilies House is a special program that provides housing designed for grandparents rearing children. It meets the unique needs of the aging grandparent and the children through a supportive service package. A third recommendation is to advocate for the exclusion of "child-only" TANF grants from the calculation of public and Section Eight housing payments. This option is already offered for children who are a part of the formal foster care system. Their foster care payment is not included in calculating their rent or total tenant payment. Generations United has also proposed conducting a nationwide survey of the housing and service needs of grandparents rearing grandchildren (Generations United, 2001).

Welfare Reform

Welfare reform forces able-bodied individuals to work without regard to their age. Although 20 percent of the households can be exempted, age is not one of the reasons cited as eligible. For individuals such as fifty-eight-year-old Willa Jones, who quit her job to care for her five grandchildren because of lack of affordable child care, the mandatory work requirement is troubling (Dornin, 1996). Thus, some older grandmothers are forced to work if they elect to be placed on the TANF grant with their grandchildren. They have already made serious sacrifices to "parent again"—this requirement forces them to also "work again."

A policy recommendation is to disregard the mandatory TANF work requirement for custodial grandparents who are caregivers. A California grandmother in the situation of finding work recommends that "there should be a separate category for grandparent caregivers because these are not our children, they are really our foster children" (Dornin, 1996, p. 2). They should neither be forced to work or remove themselves from the grant to satisfy the requirements.

SPECIAL CHALLENGES
FOR THE AFRICAN-AMERICAN COMMUNITY

The AoA encourages African-American communities and organizations to take an active role in developing state and local plans to ensure that they meet the needs of African-American elders. They encourage groups that represent elders, their families, and their service providers to voice concerns and needs through the public hearing process (AoA Fact Sheet, n.d.). It is extremely important for African-American leadership and organizations to establish a network of input to ensure that the unique needs of aging caregivers are addressed.

A content analysis of the Web sites of the major African-American organizations showed the need for increased leadership and advocacy to ensure that policies and programs like NFCSP are responsive to the needs of African-American elders in caregiving roles. As the new census data are released, it is important to use it to document disparities that can be addressed through funding priorities. It is critical for organizations to respond to the special challenges of African-American elders who are especially vulnerable because of personal, family, and societal expectations. They have to ensure that we continue the positive benefits of grandparent caregivers by bringing attention to their needs and insisting on policies that help rather than hurt.

Smith (2000) notes that the absence of consideration of how race impacts the macrostructural context of social services, public policies, and individual functioning is troubling. Further, she cites the need to examine intragroup variations. African-American leaders should be especially sensitive to the need for culturally competent research on the different cohorts of African-American elders. Identifying the particular needs of African-American grandparents and particularly grandfathers must become a priority.

Leveling the impact of double and triple jeopardy requires renewed commitment to organizations such as the National Caucus and Center for the Black Aged (NCBA). NCBA was conceived in 1971 to address the inadequate attention given to African-American elders and to take leadership in developing policies and strategies to address the unique needs of this constituency (Jackson, 1980). Meeting the challenges of the new century will require collaboration and coordination with African-American organizations and other organizations that support policies that recognize the full range of caregiver needs along the continuum of socioeconomic groups.

The nation is gearing itself for the baby boomer driven increase in the aging population. Census 2000 data show that 35 million or 12 percent of the American population are age sixty-five and over. These data show that 8.1 percent of the African-American population is sixty-five and older. The projected substantial growth of the African-American elderly population will require a new vision that addresses the needs of a group that is likely to be more economically diverse.

Thus, examining intragroup variability will become important to designing programs and delivering a new range of services for groups such as grandparent caregivers.

CONCLUSION

Our nation owes a debt of gratitude to the thousands of African-American grandparents who stand in the gap for vulnerable children. The unprecedented increase, particularly among grandfather-only and families with no parents present (Casper and Bryson, 1998), must be approached with new vision. We must be aggressive in ensuring that public policy is responsive to their needs. African Americans must be particularly vigilant to ensure that the policies that are being crafted are sensitive to the needs of older African-American grandmothers and grandfathers who are primary caregivers for grandchildren. In order to do this, a more active role must be assumed in identifying and recording the needs of this population along with the resources required for change. African-American organizations must make their constituents aware of resources available through NFCSP and launch a campaign to ensure that the most vulnerable groups are served. In addition, they must address their feelings of powerlessness by using a range of techniques including empowerment training to build on their strengths and resilience (Cox, 2002).

Guided by research that documents the continued existence of double jeopardy, new policies and practices must emerge that provide greater options and resources for grandparents who willingly serve as guardians of new generations of African Americans and other vulnerable children. Let our fortitude "to do the right thing" in the policy arena equal theirs "to do the right thing" for their grandchildren. Although public policy can never erase the double jeopardy imposed by cumulative disadvantage, it can double its efforts to put in place more policies that value their contributions.

REFERENCES

Administration on Aging [AoA] (n.d.). The national family caregiver support program. Retrieved January 18, 2002, from <http://aoa.gov/carenetwork/NFCSP-description.html>.

Administration on Aging [AoA] Fact Sheet (n.d.). *Serving our African-American Elders*.

Administration on Aging [AoA] (1997). *Grandparents as caregivers*. [Online] Available: <http://www.aoa.dhhs.gov/may97/Grandparents.html>.

American Association of Retired Persons (2001). Grandparents raising grandchildren: Where to find help. [Online] Available: <http://www.aarp.org/confacts/programs/grandraising.html>.

Angelou, M. (1994). Our grandmothers. In M. Angelou (Ed.), *The complete collected poems of Maya Angelou* (pp. 253-256). New York: Random House.

Billingsley, A. (1968). *Black families in white America*. Englewood Cliffs, NJ: Prentice-Hall.

Brown, D. and Mars, J. (2000). Profile of contemporary grandparenting in African American families. In C.B. Cox (Ed.), *To grandmother's house we go and stay* (pp. 201-217). New York: Springer Publishing Company.

Bryson, K.R. (2001). *Grandparent caregivers: New census data available*. Washington, DC: AARP.

Burlingame, V.S. (1999). *Ethnogerocounseling*. New York: Springer Publishing Company.

Burton, L.M. (1992). Black grandparents rearing children of drug-addicted parents: Stressors, outcomes, and social service needs. *The Gerontologist, 32,* 744-751.

Burton, L. and Devries, C. (1992). Challenges and rewards: African-American grandparents as surrogate parents. *Generations, 16,* 51-55. Retrieved March 26, 2001, EBSCOHOST.

Casper, L. and Bryson, K. (1998). Co-resident grandparents and their grandchildren: Grandparent-maintained families. U.S. Census Bureau, [Online] Available: <http://www.census.gov/population/www/documentation/twps0026/twps0026.html>.

Cox, C.B. (2002). Empowering African-American custodial grandparents. *Social Work, 47,* 45-54.

Dornin, R. (Correspondent). (1996, December 8). Welfare reform squeezes grandparent caregivers. San Francisco: CNN, [Online] Available: <http://www.cnn.com/US/9612/08/grandparents.welfare/>.

Feldman, C. (1997). Staying with Grandma. *Children's Advocate News Magazine,* July/August, 1-4.

Flaherty, M.J., Facteau, L., and Garver, P. (1999). Grandmother functions in multigenerational families: An exploratory study of black adolescent mothers and their infants. In R. Staples (Ed.), *The black family: Essays and studies* (pp. 223-231). Belmont, CA: Wadsworth Publishers.

Frazier, E.F. (1939). *The Negro family in the United States*. Chicago: University of Chicago Press.

Fuller-Thomson, E. and Minkler, M. (2000). African-American grandparents raising grandchildren: A national profile on demographic and health characteristics. *Health and Social Work, 20,* 109-119.

General Accounting Office (2000). *Food stamp program: Options for improving nutrition for older Americans.* RCED-00-238.

General Accounting Office (2001). *Food stamp program: Program integrity and participation challenges.* GAO-01-881T.

Generations United (1999). *Public policy agenda for the 106th Congress.* Washington, DC: Author.

Generations United (2001). *Public policy agenda for the 107th Congress.* Washington, DC: Author.

Grandparents United for Children (n.d.). Statistics on grandparent caregivers. Retrieved January 28, 2002, from <http://www.grandparentsunitedforchildren.org/GUFCR-page-statistics.html>.

Grandsplace (n.d.). U.S. Census 2000 figures on grandparents raising grandchildren. Retrieved January 18, 2002, from <http://www.grandsplace.com/gp/census2000.html>.

Greene, R. (2000). *Social work with the aged and their families.* New York: Aldine Gruyter.

Hill, R. (1997). *The strengths of African-American families: Twenty-five years later.* Washington, DC: R&B Publishers.

Hooyman, N.R. and Kiyak, H.A. (2002). *Social gerontology: A multidisciplinary perspective.* Boston: Allyn and Bacon.

Hushbeck, C. (n.d.). After welfare reform: How are grandparent caregivers managing? Retrieved March 12, 2001, from <http://www.aarp.org/grandparents/gpwelfarereform.html>.

Jackson, J.J. (1980). *Minorities and aging.* Belmont, CA: Wadsworth Publishers.

Keigher, S. and Fendt, P. (1998). Welfare at ground zero: Having to fly without a safety net. [Electronic version]. *Health and Social Work, 23,* 223-321.

Kivnick, H.Q. and Sinclair, H.M. (1996). Grandparenthood. In J.E. Birren (Ed.), *Encyclopedia of gerontology: Age, aging, and the aged,* Vol. 1 (pp. 611-623). San Diego, CA: Academic Press.

Lempert, L.B. (1999). Other fathers: An alternative perspective on African American community caring. In R. Staples (Ed.), *The black family: Essays and studies* (pp. 189-201). Belmont, CA: Wadsworth Publishers.

Mbanaso, M., Brown, C., and Ukawuilulu, J. (2002). *A study on elderly African Americans as intergenerational caregivers of aged persons: Final report.* Washington, DC: E. Franklin Frazier Center for Social Work Research: Howard University School of Social Work. Funded by Centers for Medicare and Medicaid Services.

McAdoo, H.P. (1993). *Family ethnicity: Strength in diversity.* Thousand Oaks, CA: Sage.

Minkler, M. (2001). Grandparents and other relatives raising children: Characteristics, needs, best practices, and implications for the aging network. Monograph prepared for the Lewin and the Administration on Aging. Retrieved January 18, 2002, from <http://www.aoa.gov/carenetwork/MinklerMonograph.html>.

Minkler, M., Rose, K., and Price, M. (1992). The physical and emotional health of grandmothers raising grandchildren in the crack cocaine epidemic. *The Gerontologist, 32,* 752-760.

National Association of Social Workers (2001). *Social work speaks: NASW policy statements 2000-2003* (Fifth edition). Washington, DC: Author.

National Urban League (1964). *Double jeopardy: The older Negro in America today.* New York: Author.

Pampel, F.C. (1998). *Aging, social inequality, and public policy.* Thousand Oaks, CA: Pine Forge Press.

Porterfield, J., Dressel, P., and Barnhill, S. (2000). Special situation of incarcerated parents. In C.B. Cox (Ed.), *To grandmother's house we go and stay* (pp. 184-202). New York: Springer Publishing Company.

Robertson, J.F. (1997). Should grandparents assume full responsibility? In A.E. Scharlach and L.W. Kaye (Eds.), *Controversial issues in aging* (pp. 173-184). Boston: Allyn and Bacon.

Roe, K. and Minkler, M. (1998/1999). Grandparents raising grandchildren: Challenges and responses. *Generations, 22,* 25-33.

Smith, C.J. and Beltran, A. (2000). Grandparents raising grandchildren: Challenges faced by these growing numbers of families and effective policy solutions. *Journal of Aging and Social Policy, 12,* 7-17.

Smith, J.M. (2000). Race, kinship care, and African-American children. *African American Research Perspectives, 6,* 54-64.

Takas, M. (2001). *Developing effective programs to serve grandparent-as-parent families.* AARP Grandparent Information Center. Washington, DC: Author.

U.S. Census Bureau (n.d.). Table PCT014. Grandparents responsible for own grandchildren under 18 years by sex of grandparents in households, Census 2000 Supplementary Survey Tables [Data Set]. Retrieved January 19, 2002, from <http://www.uscensus.gov>.

U.S. Census Bureau (n.d.). Table PCT019. Grandparents responsible for own grandchildren under 18 years by poverty status of grandparents in households, Census 2000 Supplementary Survey Tables [Data Set]. Retrieved January 19, 2002, from <http://www.uscensus.gov>.

U.S. Department of Health and Human Services, Administration for Children and Families (August 2000). *Temporary assistance to needy families (TANF) program: Third annual report to Congress.* Washington, DC: Author.

Whitley, D.M., Kelley, S., and Sipe, S.T. (2001). Grandmothers raising grandchildren: Are they at increased risk of health problems? *Health and Social Work, 26,* 105-115.

Chapter 4

Child Welfare Policies and African-American Families

Sandra Stukes Chipungu

America has waged two wars that have failed and left casualties in our country: the "war on poverty" and the "war on drugs." The large numbers of children served by the child welfare system and adults needing substance abuse services are evidence of the failure of these wars on major social problems. Drugs are having a devastating effect on families and children. Generations of young adults are dying due to drug overdoses, HIV/AIDS, incarceration, or violence associated with drugs. The "war on drugs" has led to an unprecedented increase in the incarceration rates for both men and women, many of whom are parents of young children (Seymour, 1998).

This chapter will provide an overview of selected major social policies in child welfare that affect African-American families and children. Selected recent child welfare policies that provide a framework for understanding child welfare are the Adoption Assistance and Child Welfare Act of 1980 (PL No. 96-272); the Adoption and Safe Families Act of 1997 (ASFA) (PL No. 105-89); the Multi-Ethnic Placement Act of 1994 (MEPA) (PL No. 103-382); the Interethnic Placement Act of 1996 (IEPA) (PL No. 104-88); the Adoption Initiative of 2002; and sections of the Personal Responsibility and Work Opportunity Reconciliation Act of 1996 (PL No. 104-193). Although these policies will be the focus of this chapter, a background of selected social problems, the prevalence of these problems, and the current status of children in child welfare will be provided.

BACKGROUND OF SELECTED PROBLEMS

The majority of poor people do not abuse or neglect their children. There are 14.1 million (19.9 percent) poor children under the age of eighteen in the United States (DiNitto, 2000). However, only approximately .5 million are in the foster care system. Children from poor families are overrepresented in child maltreatment reporting (Milner, 1994). In the United States, 688,200 cases of AIDS had been reported to the Centers for Disease Control and Prevention (CDC) as of December 31, 1998. Of these, 570,425 (83 percent) were males aged thirteen or older, 109,311 (16 percent) were fourteen years or older and 8,461 (1 percent) were children under age thirteen. From 1985 to 1998, the proportion of reported U.S. AIDS cases for women increased by 23 percent (CDC, 1998).

Nearly 1.5 million American children have a mother or father in federal or state prison, representing an increase of 500,000 since 1991 (Mumola, 2000). The Justice Department reported that 1,498,800 children under the age of eighteen have a parent in prison. This number reflects a 60 percent increase since 1991 (Seymour, 1998). The majority of children with imprisoned parents, 58 percent, were younger than ten years old, and the average age was eight years old. As of December 31, 1999, they represented 2.1 percent of the nation's 72 million minor children.

There are 8.3 million children (11 percent) who live with at least one parent who is either an alcoholic or in need of treatment for the abuse of illicit drugs. Of these, 3.8 million live with a parent who is alcoholic, 2.1 million live with a parent whose primary problem is with illicit drugs, and 2.4 million live with a parent who abused alcohol and illicit drugs in combination (USDHHS, 1999). Although figures vary, most studies show that one-third to two-thirds of children involved with the child welfare system are there due to parental substance abuse as a contributing factor. These lower figures tend to involve child abuse reports and the higher figures often refer to children in foster care (USDHHS, 1999). Parents who are alcoholic or are in need of treatment for abuse of illicit drugs are demographically quite similar to the U.S. population as a whole. Recent statistics show that the races of mothers with illicit drug use are as follows: 72 percent are white, 20 percent are black, 7 percent are Latino, and 1 percent is other (USDHHS, 1999). Mothers with substance abuse problems are much more likely to be reported to child protective services than fathers. African-American women with substance abuse problems are more likely to be involved with the child welfare system than are similar women of other races (USDHHS, 1999).

PREVALENCE OF FOSTER CARE

According to the Adoption and Foster Care Analysis Reporting System (AFCARS) Report (USDHHS, 2002), there were 556,000 children in foster care as of September 2002. The mean age of these children is 10 years and the median age is 10.1 years. Forty-eight percent of these children live in a foster family home of a nonrelative, 25 percent live in the home of a relative, 10 percent live in institutions, 8 percent live in group homes, 4 percent live in preadoptive homes, and 3 percent are in trial home visits. The mean length of stay is thirty-three months, with the median length of stay as twenty months. The permanency planning goals for these children are as follows: reunification (43 percent), other relatives (4 percent), adoption (20 percent), long-term foster care (8 percent), emancipation (5 percent), guardianship (3 percent), and not yet established (17 percent) (USDHHS, 2002). The race and ethnicity of children show that 35 percent are whites/non-Hispanic, 38 percent are black/non-Hispanic, 15 percent are Hispanic, 2 percent are Asian/Pacific Islanders, and 1 percent are Asian unknown. Fifty-two percent are boys and 48 percent are girls. During the first half of FY 2000, 146,000 children entered foster care and 124,000 exited foster care. Of those exiting foster care, 60 percent were reunited with their birth parents or primary caretaker, 11 percent were living with relatives, 15 percent were adopted, 6 percent were emancipated, 3 percent exited to guardianship, 3 percent were transferred to another agency, and 2 percent ran away. Current demographic data indicate that the number entering foster care is beginning to decline after major increases in the 1980s.

Wulczyn, Harden, and George (1994) identified several trends in foster care placement using individual administrative data on children in foster care. The study, one part of a large multistate study, examined foster care placement trends to identify changes in the size and composition of the foster care caseload over time. Among the trends noted in their analysis of substitute care rates are the following:

1. Foster care caseloads had doubled over ten years (1984-1994).
2. First time admission patterns in foster care placements are more dynamic than are exit patterns.
3. Overall, infants and young children are the fastest growing age groups in the foster care population; they are entering care in greater numbers than other groups and tend to remain in foster care longer.
4. Much of the recent growth in foster care has involved the placement of children with relatives; children in kinship placements tend to stay in care longer than children in nonrelative placements. When they do exit, kinship foster children are less likely than others to reenter care.
5. Almost two-thirds of the children who leave the child welfare system are reunified with their families. Most reunifications occur within two years of the child's initial removal from home and entry to care.
6. Approximately 10-15 percent of Archive foster children leave care to adoption. Children who enter care as infants are much more likely to become adopted than children who enter at older ages. Most adoptions occur within three to five years from the time of entry into care.
7. Although children who enter foster care will exit in a relatively timely basis, a substantial share of these children become long-term clients of the child welfare system. Over one-third of Archive children stay in care over thirty months (Wulczyn, Harden, and George, 1994).

Children who enter care as infants are more likely to become adopted than children at older ages. At first, it may appear that there is a contradiction, however these are actually two issues—adoption and entry. Infants are more likely to be adopted than older children, and they are also more likely to be brought into care. However, due to the time that it takes to adopt, these children stay in care longer.

ADOPTION ASSISTANCE AND CHILD WELFARE ACT OF 1980

The Adoption Assistance and Child Welfare Act of 1980 (PL 96-272) required states to establish programs and make procedural reforms to serve children in their homes, prevent out-of-home placement, and facilitate family reunification following placement. The Act transferred federal foster care funding from IV-A to a new Title IV-E of the Social Security Act and provided funds to help states pay adoption expenses for children whose special needs make adoption difficult (USDHHS, 2000a).

During a twenty-year period of research on foster care prior to the enactment of the law, the following problems were identified: (1) long stays in foster care, (2) unstable placements, (3) little contact between social workers and families, and (4) infrequent visits between children and their parents. Public Law 96-272 was designed to address these problems by refocusing child welfare practice on permanence for children.

A major provision of Public Law 96-272 was that judges determine whether "reasonable efforts" had been made to enable children to remain safely at home before they were placed in foster care. Reasonable efforts were also required to reunite foster children with their biological parents. Although the law required reasonable efforts to preserve and reunify families, it did not include a specific requirement for placing a child permanently in an adoptive or other permanent home (USDHHS, 2000a).

In the actual implementation of the 1980 law, some state workers interpreted the law to mean that they should work toward reunification for the first eighteen months, and if unsuccessful, they would move to terminate parental rights. This process could take another eighteen months, which resulted in some children remaining in foster care for long periods before they were freed for adoption. Thus, ASFA was passed in an effort to strengthen some of the weaknesses of the 1980 child welfare law.

1994 MULTIETHNIC PLACEMENT ACT (MEPA)

The 1994 Multiethnic Placement Act (PL 103-382) allows states to consider race and ethnicity in choosing foster and adoptive homes, but prohibits states from denying or delaying a child's placement solely on the basis of race or ethnicity. By 1996, Congress determined that the Act was not facilitating the adoption of children of color and added an amendment (PL 104-88).

The Interethnic Placement Act of 1996 (IEPA) omitted the original language that explicitly allowed agencies to consider a child's national origin, ethnicity, or race. Children of color, who make up over 60 percent of children in foster care, wait twice as long for permanent homes as do other foster children (U.S. General Accounting Office, 1998). This act sought to decrease the length of time that children wait in foster care to be adopted by eliminating what was perceived as race-related barriers to adoption. In effect, child welfare agencies were put on notice that they are subject to financial penalties for engaging in racial discrimination when making decisions related to adoption or foster care placements (Downs et al., 2000).

The most recent estimate of transracial adoption was performed in 1987 by the National Health Interview Survey (NHIS). The findings revealed that only 8 percent of all adoption included parents and children of different races. One percent of white women adopt black children. Five percent of white women adopt children of other races. Two percent of women of other races adopt white children (estimates include foreign born) (Stolley, 1993). An estimated 15 percent of the 36,000 foster children adopted in FY 1998 were transracial or transcultural adoptions (USDHHS, 2000b). The concern that the passage of MEPA would lead to an increase in transracial adoptions appears to be unwarranted. There is no single source of information on adoptions in the United States. However, there is a requirement that the number of children adopted from the public child welfare system be documented in AFCARS. In a study by the General Accounting Office (1998), the implementation of MEPA has been affected by a number of factors: (1) the need to change existing state laws, regulations, and policies; (2) the personal and professional values and beliefs of caseworkers; and (3) the challenge to the federal Department of Health and Human Services to provide policy guidance, technical assistance, training, and monitoring of compliance. Transracial adoptions remain a controversial issue in child welfare. Many social workers are professionally reluctant to make transracial placements (GAO, 1998), although they are aware that the IEPA requires that race not be considered a factor. Liederman (1998) wrote a protest letter to the Department of Health and Human Services. He stated

> We are in complete disagreement with the Department of Health and Human Service's interpretation of MEPA/IEPA as effectively disallowing any consideration of race in adoptive and fos-

ter care placement decisions. This policy directly contradicts what we know to be best practice in child welfare, and we strongly urge the Administration to modify its position in order to avoid an inadvertent disservice to children in need of families. . . . We are also extremely concerned that MEPA would undermine much needed efforts to recruit more persons of color to be adoptive parents. (p. 1)

ADOPTION INITIATIVE OF 1996

President Clinton established "Adoption 2002" in 1996, with the goal of each year doubling the number of children adopted or placed in permanent homes by 2002 (USDHHS, 1997). To meet this goal, states must modify their current procedures for moving children through the foster care system and into adoption. This goal translates into an increase in adoptions and permanent placements from 27,000 in 1996 to 54,000 in 2002. The President's Executive Memorandum focuses attention on a special group of children waiting to be adopted—the approximately 100,000 children in the public foster care system who cannot return safely to their own parents and homes. These children have often been in the foster care system for an extended period of time.

Children waiting for adoption are primarily those whose parents have been unable or unwilling to resolve the issues that precipitated placement. Of the more than 450,000 children who were in the foster care system in 1994, 100,000 could not return home without jeopardizing their health, safety, and development (USDHHS, 1997). The majority of them had a goal of adoption, with 27,000 being legally free and immediately available for adoption (USDHHS, 1997). President Clinton's FY 1998 budget sought $10 million annually for three years (FY 1998-FY 2000) to support these efforts. The Department of Health and Human Services proposed a financial bonus to states for children adopted from the public foster care system. For each child adopted over the base number for that year, a bonus would be awarded to the state. A higher bonus would be paid to the extent there are increases among children receiving Title IV-E adoption assistance. Title IV-E is the primary federal funding source for poor children in the child welfare system. It is an uncapped entitlement program that reimburses states for a portion of the cost incurred in placing children in foster care or adoptions. In FY 1995, Federal Title IV-E expenditures totaled $3 billion dollars (Geen and Waters, 1997). States have a financial incentive to increase the number of adoptions.

ADOPTION AND SAFE FAMILIES ACT OF 1997

The Adoption and Safe Families Act of 1997 (ASFA) (PL No. 105-89) made changes and clarified the policies established under the Adoption Assistance and Child Welfare Act of 1980 to help states protect and care for children in the child welfare system (USDHHS, 2000a). ASFA promotes adoption and other permanent placements for abused and neglected children who cannot be returned safely to their families. ASFA requires that the child's health and safety be the concern in making service provisions, placement, and permanency planning (USDHHS, 2000a). The key provisions of ASFA are as follows:

1. The safety of children is the paramount concern that must guide all child welfare services.
2. Foster care is a temporary setting and not a place for children to grow up.
3. Permanency planning efforts should begin as soon as a child enters the child welfare system.
4. The child welfare system must focus on results and accountability.
5. Innovative approaches are needed to achieve the goals of safety, permanency, and well-being (USDHHS, 2000a).

The mandatory changes under ASFA 1997 are as follows: First, the focus on safety; second, the twelve-month timeline for permanency hearings; third, the requirement for initiating termination of parental rights if a child is in state custody for fifteen of the most recent twenty-two months, unless the exceptions apply; fourth, health insurance for children with special needs for whom there is an adoption assistance agreement; fifth, an expanded focus on family preservation and support programs to include time-limited family reunification and adoption promotion and support services; and sixth, reports to Congress on selected issues (USDHHS, 2000a).

PERSONAL RESPONSIBILITY AND WORK OPPORTUNITY RECONCILIATION ACT OF 1996 (PRWORA)

In 1996, Congress passed the Personal Responsibility and Work Opportunity Reconciliation Act (PRWORA) (PL No. 104-193). The PRWORA repealed Aid to Families with Dependent Children (AFDC) and replaced it with Temporary Assistance to Needy Families (TANF). States have much of the responsibility for the design and administration of the TANF programs. The legislation also includes child welfare provisions. PRWORA directs states to "consider giving preference to an adult relative over a nonrelated caregiver when determining a placement for a child" (Geen and Waters, 1997, p. 3). Children in formal kinship relationships remain in the state's custody after placement. These kinship care providers generally receive some type of financial assistance for caring for a related child under AFDC. Depending upon the state policies and the specific case, formal kinship care providers receive an AFDC child-only grant, an AFDC family grant, a foster care maintenance payment, or an alternate type of grant paid by child welfare (Geen and Waters, 1997). AFDC child-only grants offer states as well as the federal government a cheaper alternative than foster care payment for formal kinship care providers.

IMPLICATIONS OF CHILD WELFARE POLICIES FOR AFRICAN AMERICANS

Shortened Timelines

The timelines for termination of parental rights is shorter than the time needed for parents to obtain and complete substance abuse treatment. It takes at least three years for a willing participant to become drug free and maintain recovery. It is important to note that not all persons in recovery for substance abuse relapse. Nearly one-third achieve permanent abstinence from their first attempt at recovery. An additional one-third have brief periods of substance use but eventually achieve long-term abstinence, and one-third have chronic relapses that result in premature death from chemical addiction and related consequences. These statistics are consistent with recovery rates of any chronic lifestyle-related illness (USDHHS, 1996). The new time lines in ASFA do provide sufficient opportunity for parents to take important steps in the recovery process, but only if treatment is quickly available. However, recovery is likely to be successful in the long term only if appropriate, quality substance abuse treatment services are provided promptly, and include aggressive outreach, retention, and monitoring as integral service components. Shortened timelines may lead to an increase in "legal orphans," children who are free for adoption but for whom no family is available to adopt.

Exclusion of Ex-Offenders

States are allowed to exclude parents convicted of felony crimes. So, if a parent has a criminal record due to drug use, he or she may become ineligible for TANF benefits, and thus would be unable to be reunified with the child. These parents would be denied the opportunity to get their children back because they will not have a source of income due to their incarceration. If a parent loses TANF benefits, he or she may also lose Medicaid benefits, which are used to pay for drug treatment. This creates a "catch-22" situation for these parents.

Child-Only TANF Grants

States are allowed to use TANF benefits in the form of child-only grants for poor children placed with relatives. States may opt to use this funding stream rather than Title IV-E because it is cheaper for the states and the federal government to fund child-only grants. This will result in the creation of a two-tiered payment system for poor children. Foster children who receive TANF receive a lower maintenance payment per month than foster children who receive Title IV-E maintenance payments. It appears that this policy is conveying the belief that poor children deserve less because their parents are poor.

Kinship Care and ASFA

When the Adoption and Child Welfare Act of 1980 was passed, forming the basis of the federal foster care law, it was almost unheard of for a child's relative to act as a foster parent. More than two million children in the United States now live in kinship care arrangements; 10 percent of these, or approximately 200,000, are foster children (USDHHS, 2000c). Currently, both ASFA and PRWORA give preferences to relatives as placements for children coming into foster care. Payments under PRWORA are lower than payments under ASFA, so kinship caregivers who provide care for their related children will remain poor. African Americans have historically cared for their kin, and they continue to do so today. However, efforts must be made to not overburden these caregivers, often aging women, who are in essence assuming the burden of larger societal problems.

Transracial Adoption

The intentions of MEPA and IEPA are to allow whites to more readily adopt African-American and other children of color (GAO, 1998). However, there are already a significant number of children of color already freed for adoption that have not been adopted. The expectation of this law and the subsequent amendments is that it will result in an increase in transracial adoptions of children of color. Whether this occurs remains to be seen. There has been an increase in adoptions—36,000 in FY 1998 to 46,000 in FY 1999. Of the 46,000 adoptions of foster children from the public foster care system, 54 percent were black, 38 percent were white, and 15 percent were Hispanic. Foster parents adopted the majority (64 percent or 29,387); 20 percent were adopted by non-relatives; and 16 percent or 7,353 were adopted by relatives. Of these adoptions, 88 percent were receiving adoption subsidies (USDHHS, 2000b).

Decrease in Recruitment of African-American Homes

These policy changes could lead to decreases in the recruitment of African-American adoptive homes. African-American organizations have shown that it is possible to recruit African-American families, but it is very difficult to ensure that they become adoptive parents (Day, 1979; Jackson-White et al., 1997). For example, only two of 800 African-American families that were recruited in a National Urban League campaign were eventually able to adopt a child (McRoy, Ogelsby, and Grape, 1997).

It seems that the assumption behind the MEPA and IEPA legislation is that the solutions for quickly having children of color obtain permanent homes is through adoption by whites. However, MEPA and IEPA may have underestimated the willingness of families to adopt all types of children regardless of their special needs. States may force regular foster parents to adopt foster children in order to qualify for the state adoption bonuses. Of the adoptions, which occurred in 1999, the majority (64 percent) were by foster parents. If we continue to convert foster homes into adoptive homes, we may decrease the number of regular foster homes available for future children who enter foster care. The long-term impact of MEPA and IEPA on African-American children in the child welfare system remains to be seen.

CONCLUSION

The numbers of children in foster care may continue to grow rather than decline despite all the permanency planning efforts of the child welfare system. These patterns will continue because the social problems leading to entry into foster care are not being solved. The child welfare system is being overwhelmed by the failure of the "war on drugs" and the "war on poverty." Because the "war on drugs" has focused on reducing consumption rather than reducing supply, the child welfare system is focused on individual behavior of substance abusing parents and their children, not the environments in which these families live. The consequences of these efforts are increasing numbers of children being placed in foster care.

The "war on poverty" has been replaced with Temporary Assistance to Needy Families rather than increases in livable wages. Poverty is directly related to the number of adults working in a household. So, as America experiences economic downturns, and unemployment rises, the poverty rates will increase.

One of the principles of ASFA is that foster care is temporary and children should be reunified with their birth families as soon as it is safe. Indeed, for 60 percent of those who enter foster care this is the result—they are reunified. However, for the remaining foster children, it may take longer for some to be reunited with their parents, while others will not be able to return home. The remaining foster children need to be placed in relative homes or adoptive homes. Some of the children in the foster care system will remain in "long-term foster care" despite the best efforts of the child welfare system. It is society's responsibility to care for and protect each child.

REFERENCES

Centers for Disease Control and Prevention (CDC) (1998). *HIV-AIDS surveillance report.* Washington, DC: Author.

Day, D. (1979). The adoption of black children: Counteracting institutional discrimination. Lexington, MA: DC Heath and Company.

DiNitto, D.M. (2000). *Social welfare: Politics and public policy* (Fifth edition). Englewood Cliffs, NJ: Prentice-Hall.

Downs, S.W., Moore, E., McFadden, E.J., and Costin, L.B. (2000). *Child welfare and family services: Policies and practice* (Sixth edition). Needham Heights, MA: Allyn and Bacon.

Geen, R. and Waters, S. (1997). The impact of welfare reform on child welfare financing. *New Federalism Series A Number A-16* (pp. 1-8). Washington, DC: The Urban Institute.

Jackson-White, G., Dozier, C.D., Oliver, J.T., and Gardner, L.B. (1997). Why African-American adoption agencies succeed: A new perspective on self-help. *Child Welfare, 46,* 239-254.

Liederman, D. (1998). Letter from David Liederman, Former CWLA Executive Director to Donna Shalala, HHS Secretary. Washington, DC: CWLA.

McRoy, R., Ogelsby, Z., and Grape, H. (1997). Achieving same-race adoptive placements for African-American children. *Child Welfare, 76,* 85-104.

Milner, J.S. (1994). Is poverty a key contributor to child maltreatment? No. In E. Gambrill and T. Stein (Eds.), *Controversial issues in child welfare* (pp. 16-28). Needham, MA: Allyn and Bacon.

Mumola, C.J. (2000, August). Incarcerated parents and their children (NCJ 182335). Washington, DC: Bureau of Justice Statistics.

Seymour, C. (1998). Children with parents in prison: Child welfare policy, policy, program, and practice issues. *Child Welfare, 77,* 469-494.

Stolley, K.S. (1993). Statistics on adoption in the United States. *Future of Children: Adoption, 3,* 26-42.

U.S. Department of Health and Human Services (1996). *Counselors' manual on relapse prevention with chemically dependent criminal offenders.* CSAT Technical Assistance Publication # 19. Rockville, MD: Author.

U.S. Department of Health and Human Services (1997). *Adoption 2002: A response to the Presidential Executive Memorandum on adoption.* Washington, DC: Author.

U.S. Department of Health and Human Services (1999). *Blending perspectives and building common ground: A report to Congress on substance abuse and child protection.* Washington, DC: Author.

U.S. Department of Health and Human Services (2000a). *A report to Congress on kinship foster care.* Washington, DC: Author.

U.S. Department of Health and Human Services (2000b). *Rethinking child welfare practice under the Adoption and Safe Families Act of 1997: Resource guide.* Washington, DC: Author.

U.S. Department of Health and Human Services (2002). *Transracial Adoption.* National Adoption Information Clearinghouse. Washington, DC: Caliber Associates. Available: <www.calib.com/naic/pubs/s_trans.cfm>.

U.S. Department of Health and Human Services. The Adoption and Foster Care Analysis and Reporting System (AFCARS) (2002). *Interim estimates for FY 2001.* Washington, DC: Author. Available: <www.acf.dhhs.gov/programs/cb/dis/afcars/cwst>.

U.S. General Accounting Office (1998). *Foster care: Implementation of the Multiethnic Placement Act poses difficult challenges.* Washington, DC: Author.

Wulczyn, F.H., Harden, A.W., and George, R. (1994). *An update from the Multistate Foster Care Data Archive: Foster care dynamics 1983-1994.* Chicago, IL: The Chapin Hall Center for Children at the University of Chicago.

Chapter 5

From Paper to People: An Analysis of Critical Welfare Reform Issues Affecting the Black Community

Sandra Edmonds Crewe

Welfare reform is one of the greatest social experiments of our time. It raises fundamental questions regarding the cause of financial dependency among thousands of individuals who are receiving welfare or are considered at risk of welfare dependency. Through embracing a "work first" philosophy, the 1996 Personal Responsibility and Work Opportunity Reconciliation Act has moved over two million families from the welfare rolls and prompted many to declare it a success. The U.S. Department of Health and Human Services' (USDHHS, 2000) *TANF Third Annual Report to Congress* states:

> These strategies of work and responsibility and rewarding families who have gone to work are paying off. Since welfare reform there has been a dramatic increase in work participation among welfare recipients. The percentage of recipients who are working reached an all time high, 33%, compared to less than seven percent in 1992 and 11% in 1996. (p. 1)

This declaration of success is corroborated by organizations such as the American Public Human Services Association (APHSA). In their report *Crossroads: Directions in Social Policy* (2001), they assert that

> In four short years, states have achieved unprecedented success implementing welfare reform, providing compelling evidence that the devolution of authority to states was indisputably the correct course of action. . . . Welfare to work is now the new pathway to independence. (pp. 25-26)

Although subsequent sections of the APHSA report focus on needed changes, the clear message is that welfare reform is a success. Other influential groups and individuals have also raised the victory flag accompanied by an anthem of success. Arkansas Governor Mike Huckabee declared that "the drop in welfare caseloads has been one of the greatest public policy successes of the century" (Cohn, 2000, p. 103). As cited by the Joint Center for Poverty Research, Representative Archer declared that "welfare reform is a success, since there are no children sleeping on grates" (Hannan and Chibucos, 1999, p. 19). The 2000 presidential campaign validated these opinions of success by failing to include welfare reform in debates and other campaign forums, thus reducing it to a nonissue.

These compelling statements from authoritative sources on the success of welfare reform weighed heavily on the 2002 reauthorization plans, yet there are some critical indicators that should focus attention on the "whole picture." In particular, the Center for Law and Social Policy (CLASP, 2002) reports that five years after the implementation of PRWORA, most states (33) reported increases in caseloads between March 2001 and September 2001. Their data also show that rolls of over twenty states have steadily increased in the past year with the average increase being just over 9 percent. While caseloads showed an overall decline of 4 percent in 2001, "the data also show, however, that in a majority of states, the number of TANF cases is increasing, particularly in the last half of 2001" (CLASP, 2002, p. 3). This trend has continued through 2002.

UNEQUAL OUTCOMES

The debate regarding the success of welfare reform is of particular relevance to the African-American community because of its growing proportion of the rolls and historically disparate social welfare policy. Thus, it is important that the African-American community add its voice to the reauthorization proposals to ensure that the rhetoric of success does not forego critical analyses of the issues within the community from its unique perspective. This often overlooked or undervalued perspective is sorely needed considering that African Americans represent the largest cohort (almost 40 percent) of Temporary Assistance to Needy Family (TANF) children (USDHHS, 2000). The DHHS 2000 Annual Report to Congress states that "the racial composition of welfare families has substantially changed in the past ten years" (p. 110). Table 5.1 shows these changes.

Shown this way, there is a decline in the proportion of African Americans on the rolls. Yet a closer look shows that the slight decrease in the percentage of African Americans is not keeping pace with the decline of white families. Furthermore, when these data are grouped differently, based upon the implementation of PRWORA, African Americans experienced an increase from 37 percent to just over 38 percent while whites declined from 36 percent to 31 percent. The USDHHS report, however, describes this as the African-American population having "trended up slightly" (p. 110) since 1996. Greater emphasis is placed on the shift from three-fifths people of color to two-thirds people of color over the past decade. This is explained in terms of increased numbers of Latinos on welfare.

Little attention is given to the potential policy implications associated with whites leaving the rolls more rapidly than other groups. The black perspective is particularly important to the analyses because it brings attention to the impact of the reform on cohorts of individuals and examines who loses and who gains as a result of the implementation of TANF. It challenges the generalization that it has been successful for all. More important, it raises questions that are needed to complete the cadre of research on welfare reform. The black perspective ensures that we look at the policy from "paper to people" and elevate the importance of "getting welfare reform right" rather than "being right about welfare reform."

This chapter presents an overview of welfare reform from the black perspective and the person-in-environment framework. It examines

TABLE 5.1. Racial and Ethnic Composition of TANF Families (Percentage)

	1990	1999	Difference
African Americans	40	38	−2
Whites	38	31	−7
Hispanics	17	25	+8
Asians	3	3.5	+.5

Source: USDHHS, 2000.

three issues that are particularly important to black communities: lifetime limits, increase in child-only cases, and the status of households who left the roll (leavers) with unknown status.

THE BLACK PERSPECTIVE AND THE PERSONAL RESPONSIBILITY AND WORK OPPORTUNITY RECONCILIATION ACT (PRWORA)

The black perspective as articulated by Howard University School of Social Work (2000) is not exclusionary; it evolves from black experiences that reflect a commitment to the history of a people and its role in meeting emerging challenges. The black perspective can be used to provide a framework for examining welfare reform that give primacy to (1) social justice, (2) the search for causes, (3) consequences and elimination of oppression, (4) the affirmation of strengths, (5) the importance and complexity of diversity, and (6) an insistence on cultural competence in addressing groups subjected to oppressive forces. A framework incorporating these principles forces a more balanced analysis of welfare reform that is equally concerned for those who have not succeeded or are experiencing marginal success. The black perspective is also compatible with a human ecological perspective in analyzing welfare reform because the discussion moves beyond self-sufficiency to sustainability and interdependency. These perspectives guide the following discussion of the 1996 Personal Responsibility and Work Opportunity Reconciliation Act (PRWORA).

PRWORA: Different Perspectives

The PRWORA (PL No. 104-193) was enacted in August 1996 and authorized through September 2002. It established the Temporary Assistance to Needy Families (TANF) program that replaced the federal entitlement program with a locally administered block grant program defined largely by a "work first" philosophy. A hallmark of TANF is its imposition of time limits to secure work and lifetime limits of up to sixty months for cash assistance. Its purpose and four objectives were to increase the flexibility of states in operating a program designed to

1. provide assistance to needy families that children may be cared for in their own homes or in the homes of relatives;
2. end the dependence of needy parents on government benefits by promoting job preparation, work, and marriage;
3. prevent and reduce the incidence of out-of-wedlock pregnancies and establish overall numerical goals; and
4. encourage the formation and maintenance of two-parent families (PRWORA, 1996, p. 2113).

The National Association of Social Workers (NASW) voiced early concern about the 1996 legislation as follows:

> It is clear that the 1996 legislation was not the result of a rational policy decision based upon a thorough review of data and experience. The destiny of poor people has been decided by opinion polls and voter bias regarding welfare recipients, rather than an informed inclusive decision making process. (NASW, 2000, p. 297)

While implicit about social justice, the NASW statement was silent on racial disparities that might surface from the reform. Although their 2002 comments on reauthorization emphasize attention to persons with multiple barriers, there is still no specific reference to racial disparities. The focus on multiple barriers clearly rejects the individual pathology rationale; yet, there is still no specific reference to race. This is perhaps a conscious effort to avoid any link between race and dependency that could evoke stereotypes of black welfare dependency. However, it seems somewhat paternalistic to omit by specific reference the obvious impact on blacks and Latinos who make up over 60 percent (1999 USDHHS data) of the rolls but less than 25 percent of the U.S. population according to Census 2000.

Welfare reform transferred important decisions to the local levels, creating opportunities for best practices to emerge within their natural setting. Devolution continued the flexibility that was begun by Aid to Families with Dependent Children (AFDC) waivers. Although applauded by many as a unique opportunity to fix the problem, many in the African-American community felt that devolution was reminiscent of states rights politics that had a history of promoting segregation and presenting legal barriers to overcome discrimination (Jeff, 1998).

African-American scholars documented their concerns about the potential for welfare reform to penalize individuals because of systemic discrimination that lingers from the de jure and de facto desegregation experienced by African Americans. Despite laws that have abolished discrimination, one can find discriminatory acts throughout the administration of public policy. To many African-American and other liberal scholars, welfare reform "ignored the realities of poverty facing our children and families" (Million Family March, Inc., 2000, p. 106). Yoo (1999) states that racism, patriarchy, and classism have influenced past and current U.S. social welfare behavior and the increasing number of black recipients on the AFDC program caused it to be attacked and promulgated the passage of the 1996 federal reform act. Although the language was color neutral, the images associated with the need to reform welfare were much too frequently African-American women. Thus, welfare reform was perceived by many as a proxy for removing blacks from the rolls (Hill, 1997).

Ethgender Effects

Welfare reform is viewed by many as a "quick fix" or "five-year fix" to a problem that has its roots in slavery. According to Gilens (1999) and Handler and Hasenfeld (1997), America has yet to erase the detrimental effects of racial discrimination inherent in social welfare policy. Karger and Stoesz (1998) similarly note that history is replete with well-intentioned social policies that have proved catastrophic. This is especially true for African Americans who have born the brunt of disadvantageous policies that give the appearance of being "color-blind." Similarly, the black community has witnessed urban renewal and affirmative action programs being prematurely dismantled or misdirected in the community. Thus, the new TANF policy was met with suspicion by many because of its ahistoricism (Burgess, 2000), or failure to address the history that caused the disproportionate numbers of African Americans to be dependent on welfare.

The ahistoric explanation (Hill, 1997) that dwelled on the individual pathology of welfare recipients failed to recognize the role of the government in oppressing African Americans and women. The ethgender effects of policies that treated women and persons of color as second-class citizens were obscured by the notion of "personal responsibility." The dual effects of racism and sexism on the economic lives of African-American women is labeled ethgender effects (Burgess, 2000). According to Murrell as cited by Burgess (2000):

> Examining ethgender effects necessitates taking into account both the unique effects of race and of sex as well as the combined effects of race by sex in accounting for economic outcomes of African American women. Thus, understanding the total effect of these factors becomes more important than partitioning which individual factors exert the greatest influence. . . . This approach should lead to the development of a holistic picture of the race, sex and ethgender effects across a variety of the outcomes of the rewards of work. (p. 175)

This is particularly important to welfare reform because the largest group of TANF recipients is now people of color, with African-American families (39 percent) being the largest cohort (USDHHS, 2000). Although the USDHHS annual report on TANF does not specifically give the number of African-American families headed by women, one can assume that a substantial majority are based upon the historical design of the program to serve women with children. Thus, the examination of welfare reform must give primacy to ethgender effects.

To many advocates of the poor, the debate surrounding welfare reform was painfully reminiscent of the controversial 1965 Moynihan report (Staples, 1999) that framed the experience of African Americans as a "tangle of pathology" resulting in welfare dependency, out-of-wedlock children, and other ills. Similar to the Moynihan report, the new welfare reform accepted only partial responsibility for the problem of escalating welfare rolls. It conceptualized the problem in terms of personal pathology and the system's role in promoting immoral behavior. With the pending reauthorization, outcomes are being packaged that give credence to the methods. President Bush stated in his reauthorization plan that the success of welfare reform had indeed proved the validity of the Moynihan report (Bush, 2002). This is perhaps one of the most distressing aspects of the reauthorization plan because it provides proof that the pejorative effects of the racialization of welfare reform are likely to continue after reauthorization. The statement clearly shows a lack of sensitivity and respect for the opinions of blacks who continue to find the Moynihan report offensive.

There has been a "rush to judgment" to declare welfare reform a success without full exploration of some important unanswered questions. Facts such as the decline of welfare rolls by 50 percent, the increase of work among single women from 57 percent to 73 percent, and the decline of poverty among children from 22 percent to 16 percent are presented as evidence of its success (Falk et al., 2001). These are impressive numbers, but do they tell the story for all sectors of the community? Do they overemphasize success at the expense of those who are still making the transition? Are their notes of caution watered down by their bolder proclamation of success?

Quality of Life

While many have focused their evaluation of welfare reform on its success in moving families from the rolls or to work, others attempt to reframe the dialogue to address quality of life issues. Quality of life is defined by Lehman (1983) as the "sense of well-being and satisfaction experienced by people under their current condition" (p. 143). The coordination between and among agencies has resulted in numbers of families being able to move from welfare to work and receive needed supports and resources. Similar to other proponents of the reform, they recognize that the success of many families is contingent upon continuation of supports such as medical assistance, transportation, child care, and housing vouchers. Although it is indisputable that many families have moved to work, it is equally indisputable that they are doing so because of the "extra" supports that many opponents insisted upon being included in the reform initiatives (APHSA, 2001; Cohn, 2000).

Policy scholars concerned with quality of life insist that the claims of success be tempered by the realities of the causes and consequences of the exodus of families from welfare to work (Child Trends, 2001; Cohn, 2000; Hannan and Chibucos, 1999; Hollar, 2001; National Partnership for Women and Children, 1999). Although most concur that the predictions of social problems such as homelessness and expanding foster care have not materialized, they quickly note that systems were put in place to address some of these concerns and that the first five years of welfare reform occurred in a robust economy. In addition, they cite an early emphasis placed on the most "employable," thus inflating the early success figures. The state of Maryland used this approach (Crewe, Schervish, and Gourdine, 2000b). Maryland's welfare reform program was specifically designed to assist those who were most job ready to exit welfare first. This approach was adopted to create program savings from early leavers that could be used to serve families who were expected to experience more difficulty. The current data show a much more subdued exodus to work. This supports the existence of early strategies aimed at more employable individuals.

Quality of life proponents point to the importance of moving families out of poverty. The fact that most are receiving wages in excess of minimum wage does not address the inadequacy of the wages to support their living expenses and move them to states of self-sufficiency. Thus quality of life proponents are clear in their position that the past five years of TANF implementation is the first chapter and not the epilogue to welfare reform (Child Trends, 2001). They feel that at best welfare reform void of measures of well-being represents a pyrrhic victory because it does not address the higher goal of eliminating poverty (Jansson, 2001). Quality of life proponents credit the beginning success of welfare reform with companion policies and programs that focused on making work pay and providing needed supports such as child care (Besharov and Germanis, 2000).

The Undeserving Poor

The PRWORA, through its time limits and sanctions, has already begun to further bifurcate the poor along lines of "deservingness" and has created new potentially pejorative labels such as "deadbeat dads," "wall hitters," and "hard core" to describe those who are unsuccessful. In assessing the individual's failure to comply, inadequate attention is given to the lack of caseworker support that "results in situations in which recipients lose much needed benefits due to technicalities that could have been avoided with better information" (Walters and DeWeever, 1999, p. 31). Systemic barriers are often camouflaged by the labels justifying sanctions, thus negating the need to examine the underlying reason an individual's lack of movement toward self-sufficiency. The following quote from a report titled *Time Out!* is representative of this perspective.

> Thousands of TCA [TANF] customers have accepted their responsibility to search for work, attend work activities, abide by the myriad of rules governing their behavior as a condition of re-

ceiving benefits. They cannot take personal responsibility for a bureaucracy that has been slow to tackle its own responsibilities to provide supportive services, nor for a local economy that simply cannot produce enough jobs. Of these three actors—the economy, the bureaucracy, and the welfare customer—only the customer has been placed under time limit to perform or face stark consequences. (Family Investment Program Legal Clinic, 1999, p. 37)

This more radical perspective cautions about the possibility of "re-segregation" induced by a sanctioned driven welfare reform.

MULTIDIMENSIONAL POLICY FRAMEWORK

These different perspectives on welfare reform document the need for policy analysis to be multidimensional. It is not sufficient to focus on how many individuals leave the rolls. The analysis must address the reasons for success and failure and recognize the challenge of many U.S. social policies to correct lifelong race-based inequities. Ultimately, meaningful evaluations of welfare must examine quality of life for cohorts of individuals as it evolves from "paper to people." This can only be done through direct dialogue with individuals whose real lives are affected by our paper policies and by asking questions important to the black community that either remain unanswered, partially answered, or unasked.

Chambers (1993) cautions that there is no such thing as the "right" or "only true" social problem viewpoint and that the way social problems are understood is highly variable and depends on the viewer. Thus, the outcome of a social problem or policy is inextricably linked to the definition of the problem. It is this understanding that offers insight into the differences between blacks and whites, Democrats and Republicans, and liberals and conservatives in examining the success of welfare reform. Although there was general consensus among these groups that the "old welfare system" needed an overhaul, the specifics of what needed changing was at the crux of the debate.

Those who framed the question in terms of individual abuse, pathology, and rising costs are more likely to point to the success of falling rolls. Similarly, those concerned with the pre-TANF racialization of the rolls are more likely to cite its success. Those concerned with the postracialization and disparate impact of PRWORA on persons of color are more prone to see it as a failure. Finally, those who viewed the changes as a means to end poverty are likely to be less impressed with the statistics on the changing demographics of the rolls and more focused on the outcomes after a recipient leaves the rolls.

A value-based evaluation of welfare reform will help to ferret out policy problems using an explicit set of criteria that identifies problematic policy and program features (Chambers, 1993). According to Chambers, the value critical approach recognizes that social problem costs (losses) are not equally shared among citizens and asks and answers the question who loses the most. This is congruent with the black perspective that gives primacy to social justice and searches for underlying causes to social problems using an ecological perspective that minimizes the role of individual pathology. The following three critical aspects of welfare reform are discussed using the black perspective: time limits, child-only cases, and lost recipients.

Time Limits

> Welfare reform is unfair to people of color because they discriminate against us and do not give us enough help in finding a job. Yet, we are required to get out and benefit within a short time frame. (Crewe, Schervish, and Gourdine, 2000b, p. 42)

The question that begs an answer is "At the end of sixty months, are African Americans at greater risk of exhausting federal benefits?" The data show that all races and ethnic groups have not experienced welfare reform equally. Juxtaposed to the nationwide 60 percent reduction in rolls is the fact that there has been an increase in the proportion of African Americans and Latinos who remain on the rolls. In addition, the only group that has declined in proportion of those remaining on the rolls is whites. The Joint Center on Political and Economic Studies (2001) concurs that declines in welfare caseloads may be greater in areas with greater economic opportunity, thus implying that those remaining on the rolls are more likely to be concentrated in distressed neighborhoods. According to their data, "urban counties containing the 30 largest cities had about 20% of the U.S. population throughout the 1990s. But they accounted for 39% of welfare recipients in 1998, up from 33% in 1994" (p. 7). Thus, the perspectives of

African Americans are central to the discussion of welfare reform because of the disparate impact on their communities.

The *TANF Third Annual Report to Congress* (USDHHS, 2000) recognizes this shift yet minimizes its racial impact. The executive summary states that:

> Examining demographic trends over the decade suggests that certain aspects of the caseload have been changing and that most of these changes were larger since 1996. The caseload is now made up of a greater proportion of [people of color] (most of this mirrors the growing proportion of the overall population that is Hispanic), somewhat older parents with somewhat older children, and a substantially higher proportion of cases where no adult receives assistance. (p. 3)

Other reports have also minimized or ignored the growing proportion of African Americans on welfare rolls. However, the shift to urban centers is clearly a shift in proportion of African Americans remaining on the rolls and subject to the loss of benefits because of lifetime limits. Central cities lag in decreasing welfare rolls because of a greater incidence of poverty, low skills, multiple barriers, fewer resources, lack of work experience, and more costly interventions required to assist families with multiple barriers (Meyers, 2001). Although race is not mentioned in the Meyers report, central cities are also more likely to serve women of color. This report specifically examines the experience of the District of Columbia and Baltimore, Maryland, and states that "the central city double whammy of less resources available and greater expense for services will require hard policy choices for area officials as the five-year TANF family cash assistance limits begins to be felt" (p. 1).

A substantial share of TANF recipients have characteristics that make employment difficult, such as "substance abuse, poor mental or physical health, disability, low educational attainment, limited work experience, limited English proficiency, low basic skills, or exposure to domestic violence" (GAO, 2001, p. 5).

This study also fails to link race and the "hard to employ status." The United States General Accounting Office (GAO) stated that the research studies considered reliable did not support differences based on race. This is in part because of insufficient state level data. Other less rigorous research not included in the study did identify racial differences (C. Mrena, personal communication, October 15, 2001). It is recommended that the U.S. Department of Health and Human Services (HHS) promote research and provide guidance for states to better identify hard to employ TANF recipients who will reach sixty-month federal time limits. The challenge of serving the population that remains on the TANF rolls after the first implementation period is that they fall in multiple categories including those experiencing domestic violence, physical and developmental disabilities, substance abuse, mental health problems, learning disabilities, and other undiagnosed problems. They have not qualified for an exemption, yet they have not found work. To effectively address their needs, programs will need to use a mix of policies that encompass not only different policies but different levels of intensity to address problems (Gilbert, 1999). There must be both breadth and depth in policy flexibility.

Data from the *TANF Third Annual Report to Congress* also indicate that thirty-seven states assess and screen for these barriers to employment and fewer than half (twenty-four states) have intensive counseling (USDHHS, 2000). A TANF client describes it this way:

> [They] need qualified workers. Reform is working for worker's ego and finances and not clients. Workers are receiving incentives (money) to rush people off welfare. The workers subsequently are not attempting to identify needs of clients. But are looking to deny needed services without due process. (Crewe, Schervish, and Gourdine, 2000b, p. 47)

The fate of these individuals may lie with the decision making of frontline workers on whether they are "worthy" or "deserving" of the state option to extend benefits. Understanding the importance of planning for individuals with barriers, federal agencies issued guides, best practices, and innovative programs to stimulate new thinking. The analysis of the TANF gainers and losers signals that the African-American community is disproportionately at risk of benefit termination if the TANF rules are not changed to address their needs. Labels such as "hard to serve, wall hitters, hard to employ, multiply challenged" have the potential to stigmatize them. APHSA (2001) cautions that defining "hard-to-serve" has both advantages and disadvantages because of its potential to identify and stigmatize individuals.

The issue of the adequacy of the 20 percent hardship exemption becomes extremely important for the group assumed to have barriers placing them at risk of successfully navigating the welfare system. According to PRWORA (1996), a hardship exemption may exempt a family from the sixty-month lifetime limit for federal TANF assistance for reason of hardship or if the family is subjected to domestic violence or extreme cruelty. The exemption is in effect per fiscal year and is restricted to 20 percent of the average monthly number of families within the state.

Child-Only Cases

The substantial increase in "child-only" cases is another significant change affecting the black community. There are several unanswered questions: Why are there more cases? Who are they? How are these families and children faring? Although the research is sparse on these cases, one can surmise that quality of life is not improved for many of these children. It is clear that the increase in child-only cases indicates that welfare reform in some part has failed in its fourth objective to encourage the formation and maintenance of two-parent families.

In an effort to better understand the issues of "child-only" cases, the author conducted a focus group of black grandparents in Maryland who were heads of household for child-only TANF cases. In the focus group, consisting of ten grandparents ranging from age forty-nine to sixty-three, the grandparents spoke about the added stress of caring for grandchildren and the hardships, such as lacking financial resources for food, clothing, and health care. These are some of their comments (Crewe, 2001):

- We've put our life on the back burner to raise these children.
- I can't get food stamps because they think I am going to eat the food.
- Babysitters get $140 a week and we get $340 monthly from TANF.
- I've been on my job thirty-two years. I would like to retire, but I can't quit because I need to work for five grandchildren.

An analysis of the USDHHS statistical reports shows a 6 percent increase for forty-nine states that reported child-only cases (USDHHS,

2000). This represents almost 30 percent of the aggregate caseload. A partial explanation is that some states have reclassified prior AFDC cases into kinship care. This reclassification is described as a "policy obfuscation" (Keigher and Fendt, 1998, p. 226) aimed at reducing welfare rolls by converting them to other forms of public assistance.

Other shifts may relate to individuals abandoning efforts to conform to rules. Crewe, Schervish, and Gourdine (2000b) documented that 67 percent of TANF individuals had problems with depression and 33 percent of those with problems were clinically depressed using the Hudson's Generalized Contentment scale. Snowden, Dimas, and Vega (1999) also document that the proportion of TANF mothers meeting DSM-IV standards clearly exceeds the 20 percent exemption from the five-year lifetime eligibility limit. Individuals experiencing depression may be unable to cope with the multiple stressors caused by the pressure to work and having to leave their children with their parents or other relatives. Untreated depression caused by multiple stressors may add to the explanation of the growing child-only rolls.

The danger of the growing number of child-only households is the extra burden they place on already fragile households. Adding children to some households can add strain to an already extended budget. Although caregivers generally accept their responsibility and carry it out with love, many complain that they are not valued.

Leavers with Unknown Status

A final question that eludes an answer in the plethora of welfare reform research is "What has happened to the substantial number of persons who have left the rolls and are not working?" Who are they? Between 50 to 70 percent of families who left the rolls are working (USDHHS, 2000). This suggests that between 30 and 50 percent who exited the rolls are not employed. Little data are available on the individuals who are not reported to be working. There is anecdotal information that they may be employed in informal ways such as personal services that are not reported. Others may simply have become discouraged and are relying upon others to supply their needs.

Crewe, Schervish, and Gourdine (2000b) surveyed 200 TANF recipients (90 percent African American) and found that over 40 percent of TANF recipients did not know when their time limit was up. In addition, only 40 percent indicated that they understood welfare reform changes. Just over 25 percent stated that they had little or no understanding of the welfare changes. A concerned 22 percent stated that they did not believe that they could accomplish what was asked of them. Also, a staggering 65 percent stated that they did not know how long they could receive other benefits like food stamps, medical assistance, and child care vouchers. This finding is corroborated by the documented 33 percent plunge in food stamp rolls since the implementation of TANF. The decline in food stamp participation offers further evidence that many families do not understand the potential full range of benefits (Cohn, 2000), and that this population is vulnerable to stress and unchecked role strain.

POLICY IMPLICATIONS

Research

Section 413 of Public Law No. 104-193 calls for research to be conducted on the benefits, effects, and costs of operating the different state programs. In addition, the studies address effects of programs on such social problems as teen pregnancy, child well-being, and employment rates. Although there is a wide array of research studying various aspects of welfare reform, more culturally competent research is needed. Culturally competent research will acknowledge and respect the importance of culture in the collection and dissemination of research (Lum, 2000). Because of the disparate impact of TANF on families of color (Gooden, 1998), African Americans must insist on getting data on the aforementioned questions. We cannot settle for incomplete answers and dismissal of data from community-based research that fails the rigor of experimental design. While evidence-based research using randomized samples is valuable and desirable, we must still use the evidence produced by collective narratives obtained from smaller research projects. It is this type of research that often voices the impact of the paper on the people. According to Witkin and Harrison (2001),

> We learn to listen for discrepancies between the public discourse of disadvantaged people dealing with more powerful systems and the internal discourse within groups and individuals that frequently offer different understandings. In this sense

social workers are cultural bridges, able to deal in the multiple worlds of understanding. Sometimes this involves using the logic of EBP [Evidence Based Practice] with clients when there is credible evidence of some relevant knowledge available. Other times, however, the most important work is in educating decision makers or those who have control of the resources about how irrelevant the best scientific evidence is to the world of people whose experiences brought them into contact with the professionals. (p. 294)

Thus welfare reform research must lend itself to elements of cultural competence that value diversity in methods and authors. Fook (1996) cautions that while we champion research that meets certain scientific rigor, we cannot ignore products of the reflective researcher who seeks a more holistic approach to ensure that a congruent picture of the way people experience the world is expressed.

TANF recipients often ask social workers to look at the holistic picture before passing judgment on his or her deservingness of assistance. As the reauthorization debate ensues, the question will ultimately be raised whether welfare reform is a success. We must resist the simple answer that often leads to characterizing it as a "smashing success" (Cohn, 2000, p. 103) and reflect upon the experiences of clients. Ultimately, the reauthorization should be based upon an understanding of those who have and have not been well served. This approach elevates the needs before applauding the success.

Time Limits

Time limits and sanctions must be evaluated to ensure that they do not have a disparate impact on persons of color. Data must be produced in a way that we can determine the racial profiles of households that are sanctioned or have benefits terminated for reasons other than employment. In addition, there must be recognition that individuals who are forced to leave the rolls are not a single group. As noted, many represent various segments of the population who have complex problems, such as clinical depression, that are not properly addressed at the local level. Thus five-year time limits may be unreasonable for some families and the 20 percent exemption may not meet their needs in the next five years. This is very probable given the downturn in the economy. Evidence suggests that rolls in areas with a slow economy have not experienced the decline which stronger economic areas have seen. For example, there was an 88 percent increase in Guam's rolls from 1993-2000. A TANF recipient from Guam raises the question, "How can it be a success when there are no jobs in Guam?" (M. V. Valoria, personal communication, July 30, 2001). Similarly, other localities are reporting increased rolls with declining economic strength.

Some recipients have already reached time limits without being prepared for long-term employment (GAO, 2001). In addition, some of the states concluded that although they are currently able to meet the needs of hardship cases through the 20 percent exemption,

> as caseloads continue to fall, the number the state can provide with extended benefits will also fall . . . at some point, even families facing severe hardship will have their federal benefits terminated because they cannot be served by the current 20 percent hardship exemption policy. (p. 30)

This quote points to the need for the reauthorization to provide more flexibility in the 20 percent hardship exemption policy and monitor cases that are terminated to ensure that those involved are not victims of street level bureaucracy (Lipsky, 1980) and other disparate policy practices. Before finalizing sanctions and terminations, partnerships should be formed with outside entities that are culturally competent to ensure that needs are properly assessed and services made available and accessible.

Sanctioning

Sanctioning is another aspect of welfare reform that African Americans should carefully scrutinize. Although wide state-level variation occurs in the number of families sanctioned, sanctioned clients generally have more barriers to employment than nonsanctioned families and are more likely to have problems understanding the rules. The Welfare Information Network (1999) has also found little evidence that full family sanctions improve program compliance. In fact, they report that an increased stress level and other mental health problems are the most common impacts of sanctions. These findings should cause alarm in the African-American community as some of the states with larger African-American populations have the highest sanction levels (USDHHS, 2000). For example, in 1999, of the 13,481 TANF families in Mississippi, 85 percent were black and 22 percent of these individuals had been sanctioned. Similarly, Florida reported a 73 percent African-American and Latino population and a 32 percent sanction rate. Each of these states report a higher sanction than employment rate (USDHHS, 2000). Data from cities and counties may suggest even greater race-based disparities in sanctioning. Thus, future research must examine the race and ethnicity of sanctioned clients to ensure that the practice is not subject to ethgender bias.

The Dilemma of Frontline Workers

As with any policy, there are some individuals who will seek ways of "getting over." There is no dispute that this happens. Frontline workers quickly point out individuals who expend more energy trying to avoid compliance than they do in utilizing available resources to lead them out of poverty. These workers are concerned with the effect of policy changes that undo the progress by an overly liberal response to those who have not complied. They recognize the duplicity of some clients and struggle to discriminate between those who need help and those who abuse help. Clients need the help of culturally competent professionals who can help them respond to the monumental challenge that has been thrust upon them to fix a system in five years that has been broken for decades. They need help to work with clients who need respect and a service approach that shows appreciation for the underlying causes of the dependency.

Increased flexibility is only effective with increased knowledge of working with complex cases. These workers remind us of how life is in "the real world" as opposed to the "paper world" of welfare reform. Securing and training professional social workers to deal with the new complexities of welfare reform should be a vital part of the reauthorization debate. This is essential if the reform is to address self-sufficiency and quality of life.

Upgrading the Vision to Quality of Life

Perhaps the best change that could be made during reauthorization is philosophical. Quality of life should replace the "personal responsibility" emphasis. A "Quality of Life" bill places primacy on creating a system that moves individuals from welfare to an improved quality of life. The stressors associated with working mothers who are sometimes compromising the safety of their children to work must be addressed. If moving to work means families are struggling to make ends meet, then success has eluded us. One mother explains her struggle this way:

> I don't appreciate how your assistance works for some people. I'm a honest hardworking individual and as soon as I got a paycheck, you all decided to cut everything and I've had a long rough road in front of me ever since. I was under the impression that your program was temporary to help you get stable and on your feet. Well, I guess I was wrong. (Crewe, Schervish, and Gourdine, 2000a)

Solely having a strong work ethic does not ensure equal outcomes for all. Persistent inequalities result in unequal outcomes (Rothman, 1993). Thus, the system must work to continue the success that it claims by ensuring that working leads to an increased quality of life. A livable wage, a quality home, a quality neighborhood, appropriate child care, affordable health care, and increased education are important to judging welfare reform as a success. Jencks (1992) asks that we rethink social policy by focusing on making low-wage work economically attractive. This approach is more likely to gain support because it reinforces rather than subverts the work ethic. According to a Child Trends Research Brief (2001), welfare reform is only the first step of what may be "a long, arduous, and complex journey" (p. 1) to eradicating child poverty. Cohn (2000) suggests that the only way to make welfare a success is for Congress to make sure that recipients are getting needed benefits after their welfare checks are replaced with payroll checks. A substantial proportion of former TANF recipients report serious economic difficulties and financial strain (Danziger et al., 2000). This validates the importance of the Clinton strategy of maximizing the success of welfare reform by making work pay.

Now is the time to advocate for the abandonment of the misguided assumption that provisions of benefits discourages work (Hannan and Chibucos, 1999). Hollar (2001) advocates that "informed policy activity around TANF reauthorization in 2002 also demands a quality of life focus" (p. 30). Without it she and others argue that public administrators and policy makers do not have the broad range of information necessary to make informed and culturally competent decisions about this important social policy. To gain accurate data on quality of life, a client-researcher partnership is essential to make client views clear (Greenley, Greenberg, and Brown, 1997).

CONCLUSION

African Americans cannot afford to be silenced by the resounding proclamation of successes of welfare reform. To do so conflates success with roll reduction. Those that have used welfare reform to improve their lives must be encouraged to advocate for needed support services. Simultaneously, we must look to the citizens who are least served and ensure a safety net is available for them. This effort must happen at multiple levels. Researchers, scholars, practitioners, and clients must collaborate to tell the "real" story using various research methods and populations. Policymakers must seek data that provide a more holistic explanation of outcomes, both the bitter and the sweet (Schiele, 1998).

The opportunities that TANF reauthorization present must be informed by and speak to varied research findings. It must go beyond what is documented on paper to what is on the face of those who have "been reformed" and those "yet to be reformed." As culturally competent policymakers, our words should be undergirded by a history that reminds us of the sacrifices of many to enable us to have a voice. According to Jeff (1998), "History has proven that each time America has nationalized a scheme to degrade and exclude, or at least forward policies not in the best interest of the African American, Black ingenuity results, and new opportunities emerge" (p. 54). An understanding of this strength perspective allows us to assume a voice that addresses welfare reform from a black perspective and use it as a stage to promote social justice and quality of life.

African Americans are unique in the ability to discuss the needs of individuals and communities without pathologizing, stereotyping, or patronizing them. While we are not and should not be in lockstep, the range of our political philosophies should be combined to present a balanced perspective on the impact of welfare reform on the African-American community and other oppressed groups. Ultimately, to declare welfare reform a success for all people, it must be redesigned to a quality of life agenda that respects disparities caused by racism and shifts the focus from paper to people.

REFERENCES

American Public Human Services Association [APHSA] (2001). *TANF hard to serve.* Retrieved December 5, 2002, from <http://www.aphsa.org/monograph. pdf>.

Besharov, D. and Germanis, P. (2000). Welfare reform—four years later. [Electronic version] Welfare Academy <http://www.welfareacademy.org/pubs/four_yea.cfm>.

Burgess, N.J. (2000). Sociohistorical perspectives. In N. J. Burgess and E. Brown (Eds.), *African-American women: An ecological perspective* (pp. 5-14). New York: Falmer Press.

Center for Law and Social Policy (CLASP) (2002). *CLASP update.* January. Available online at <http://www.clasp.org>.

Chambers, D.E. (1993). *Social policy and social programs.* New York: Macmillan Publishing Company.

Child Trends (2001). *Working poor families with children: Leaving welfare doesn't necessarily mean leaving poverty* (Research Brief). May. Washington, DC: Author.

Cohn, L. (2000). From welfare to worsefare. [Electronic version] *Business Week,* 3702, 103-105.

Crewe, S.E. (2001). Welfare reform—grandparent caregiver focus group. Unpublished raw data.

Crewe, S.E., Schervish, P., and Gourdine, R.M. (2000a). Risks and resiliency open-ended comments. Unpublished raw data.

Crewe, S.E., Schervish, P., and Gourdine, R.M. (2000b). *Welfare reform: Risk and resilience indicators of TCA customers in Prince George's County, Maryland.* Washington, DC: Howard University E. Franklin Frazier Research Center.

Danziger, S., Corcoran, M., Danziger, S., and Heflin, C. (2000). Work, income, and material hardship after welfare reform. [Electronic version]. *Journal of Consumer Affairs, 34,* 6.

Falk, G., Burke, V., Gish, M., Soloman-Fears, C., Richardson, J., and Spar, K. (2001). *Welfare reform reauthorization: Brief summary of issues of 107th Congress.* [RS20766] January. Congressional Research Service. Washington, DC: Library of Congress.

Family Investment Program Legal Clinic (1999). *Time out! A status on welfare reform in Baltimore city at the three-year mark, as experienced by those it was intended to help and their legal advocates.* Baltimore, MD: Author.

Fook, J. (1996). *The reflective researcher.* Australia: Allen and Unwin.

Gilbert, N. (1999). Welfare reform and the hard-to-serve. *Social Welfare Policy at Berkeley, 7,* 10-11.

Gilens, M. (1999). *Why Americans hate welfare.* Chicago: University of Chicago Press.

Gooden, S.T. (1998). All things not being equal: Differences in caseworker support toward black and white welfare clients. *Harvard Journal of African Americans Public Policy, 4,* 23-43.

Greenley, J.R., Greenberg, J.S., and Brown, R. (1997). Measuring quality of life: A new and practical survey instrument. *Social Work, 42,* 244-254.

Handler, J.F. and Hasenfeld, Y. (1997). *We the poor people: Work, poverty, and welfare.* New Haven: Yale University Press.

Hannan, K.L. and Chibucos, T.R. (1999). *Welfare reform, poverty, and families with young children.* June. Joint Center for Policy Research Working Paper Series. Available online: <www.jcpr.org>.

Hill, R. (1997). *The strengths of African-American families: Twenty-five years later.* Washington, DC: R&B Publishers.

Hollar, D. (2001). *A holistic theoretical model for examining welfare reform: Quality of life* (Harvard Family Research Project at Harvard University). Boston, MA: Harvard University.

Howard University School of Social Work (2000). *Field instruction manual of the master of social work program.* October. Washington, DC: Author.

Jansson, B. (2001). *The reluctant welfare state: American social welfare policies—past, present, and future* (Fourth edition). Pacific Grove, CA: Brooks/Cole.

Jeff, M.F.X. (1998). The National Association of Black Social Workers' reflection on the new welfare reform law. *Harvard Journal of African American Public Policy, 4,* 49-58.

Jencks, C. (1992). *Rethinking social policy: Race, poverty and the underclass.* New York: Harper Perennial.

Joint Center for Political and Economic Studies (2001). *Devolution.* Washington, DC: Author. Available online: <http://130.94.20.119/devolution>.

Karger, H. and Stoesz, D. (1998). *American social welfare policy* (Third edition). New York: Longman, Inc.

Keigher, S. and Fendt, P. (1998). Welfare at ground zero: Having to fly without a safety net. *Health and Social Work, 23,* 223-321.

Lehman, A.F. (1983). The effects of psychiatric symptoms on quality of life assessment among the chronically mentally ill. *Evaluation and Program Planning, 6,* 143-151.

Lipsky, M. (1980). *Street-level bureaucracy.* New York: Russell Sage Foundation.

Lum, D. (2000). *Social work practice and people of color.* Belmont, CA: Brooks/Cole Publishing.

Meyers, C.S. (2001). *The District and Baltimore face double whammy in welfare reform: Greater challenges and less funding for needed services.* Washington,

DC: The Brookings Institution. Available online: <http://www.brook.edu/es/urban/gwrp/welfare_double_whammy_fullreport. htm>.

Million Family March, Inc. (2000). *The national agenda: Public policy issues, analyses, and programmatic plan of action 2000-2008.* Washington, DC: Author.

National Association of Social Workers (2000). *Social work speaks: NASW policy statements 2000-2003.* Washington, DC: Author.

Personal Responsibility and Work Opportunity Act of 1996 (PRWORA), 42 USC, Public Law. No. 104-193, 110 Stat. 2105.

Rothman, R.A. (1993). *Inequality and stratification: Class, color, and gender* (Second edition). Englewood Cliffs, NJ: Prentice-Hall.

Schiele, J. H. (1998). The Personal Responsibility Act of 1996: The bitter, the sweet for African-American families. *Families in Society, 79,* 424-429.

Snowden, L., Dimas, J.M., and Vega, W.A. (1999). Mental health needs of Mexican American mothers on welfare. *Social Welfare Policy at Berkeley, 7,* 11-12.

Staples, R. (1999). *The black family: Essays and studies.* Belmont, CA: Wadsworth Publishing Company.

U.S. Department of Health and Human Services, Administration for Children and Families (2000). *Temporary Assistance to Needy Families (TANF) Program: Third annual report to Congress.* August. Washington, DC: Author.

U.S. General Accounting Office (2001). *Welfare reform: Moving hard-to-employ recipients into the workforce.* GAO-01-368. March. Washington, DC: Author.

Walters, R.W. and DeWeever, G.E. (1999). *In their own words: Community activists discuss welfare and health care reform.* The Scholar Practitioner Program, University of Maryland.

Welfare Information Network (April 1999). Use of sanctions under TANF. *Issue Notes,* 3(3). [Electronic version] Retrieved May 31, 2001, from <http://www.welfareinfo.org/sanctionsissuenotes.htm>.

Witkin, S.L. and Harrison, D. (2001). Whose evidence for what purpose? *Social Work, 46,* 293-296.

Yoo, G.J. (1999). Racial inequality. Welfare reform and black families: The 1996 Personal Responsibility and Work Opportunity Reconciliation Act. In R. Staples (Ed.), *The black family* (pp. 357-366). Belmont, CA: Wadsworth Publishing Company.

Chapter 6

The Policy Implications of the Surgeon General's Report on Mental Health, Race, Culture, and Ethnicity

King E. Davis

In his autobiography, Quincy Jones (2002), the noted musician and arranger, describes a series of tragic events that culminated with his mother being hospitalized in a state institution for the mentally ill in 1941, when he was seven years of age. Jones and his younger brother witnessed his mother's progressive psychiatric decomposition, the profound and puzzling changes in her personality, and the marked deterioration of her personal appearance. Sarah Jones, a young woman of great beauty and musical talent, became consumed by unpredictable "spells" (p. 2), accompanied by outbursts of anger and accusations. Subsequent to her "spells" her family and neighbors watched her cyclical pattern of involuntary admissions to the care of the state, followed by short-lived escapes (p. 10). Jones recalls that after many years of failed efforts to obtain treatment to arrest her illness and lead to her recovery, his father decided to abandon his mother by leaving her in the state mental institution in Illinois while moving Jones and his younger brother back and forth from Chicago to St. Louis, Louisville, and eventually to Seattle. Feeling frustrated by his chronically mentally ill wife, Jones' father assumed that by moving some distance away he would be able to protect his young sons from their mother's frenetic behavior and from the communal shame and stigma that accompanied the drastic changes in her personality, behavior, functioning, and appearance. However, within a few years, Jones' mother located her family, but she was never able to regain her previous high level of functioning or the social standing and esteem that she once had within her family, neighborhood, and church as a competent, caring, highly educated, and talented black woman.

Over the years, Sarah Jones sought to reestablish her role in her family but her frequent relapses and the residual effects of chronic schizophrenia challenged and threatened her former husband, his new spouse, and her children. Jones' description of and response to her illness suggests that he, his father, his younger brother, neighbors, and other relatives never clearly grasped or understood the meaning of severe mental illness (paranoid schizophrenia), its probable causes, or standard treatment approaches. Jones' father, too, seemed unclear and unaware of how to advocate for quality care for his wife, how to maintain her dignity, or how to remain actively involved in her treatment. He seemed sorely overwhelmed, ashamed, impotent, and defeated by the mystery of her persistent and unremitting mental illness and by the complexity of public policies and systems that were offered. Long-term institutionalization, often involuntarily, in state hospitals with limited and unsatisfactory results appeared to have been the singular option available to Jones' family. However, it is clear that the public mental health system in Illinois in 1941 (or in any other state for that matter) had minimal scientific understanding, knowledge, or interest in the role of Sarah Jones' African-American culture in either restoring her health or its probable linkages to her illness. Nor was it clear how to incorporate the strengths that her environment offered to her well-being or potential recovery. At that time, each of these state systems operated on knowledge that tended to reflect the prevailing racial views in the society and in psychiatry (Thomas and Sillen, 1972). Blacks were considered inferior mentally as well as socially in American cities and in state mental hospital systems.

Over the course of many years, Quincy Jones and his brother saw further decomposition in their mother's mental status and periodically distanced themselves from her unpredictable and somewhat bizarre behavior until later in her life. In his personal eulogy at his brother's funeral, Quincy Jones concludes that his mother's debilitating and confusing illness, occurring at such an early and vulnerable time in their lives, robbed he and his brother of the opportunity to have an emotionally healthy parent who could have reinforced their collective sense of self-worth and accomplishment. Jones believes that the loss of his mother established personal barriers that were never resolved throughout his brother's life. It appears too that Sarah Jones did not recover from her psychiatric losses and remained mentally disabled until her death. In so many ways, the Jones' family and their neighbors did not recover from the lifelong grief, stigma, personal sense of loss, and myths that were associated with Sarah Jones' difficult-to-understand illness.

It seems likely that Sarah Jones' illness was experienced by her neighbors, who were also involuntarily hospitalized with a stigmatizing diagnosis of severe mental illness, in an all-too-available state institution. Historically, most of those committed from black communities have been men (Ramm, 1989). Once hospitalized, many of these low income black men remained in the state institution for a significant portion of their lives; but, the diagnosis and treatment they received lacked a clear understanding of the probable linkages between race, culture, ethnicity, and mental illness amidst the dim prospects of cure and recovery. In all too many instances, the diagnosis of severe mental illness was a clinical error based on a lack of cultural competence. Their families and neighbors were impotent to change, influence, or participate in the formulation of public policies or the court procedures that placed them in lifelong institutions for the mentally disabled. Sometimes the only recourse for these families was to use an informal means to manage an illness or perhaps delay or ignore their need for psychiatric services until a catastrophe forced an appeal for assistance from the police.

Close to sixty years after Quincy Jones' mother was diagnosed with an enigmatic and confusing illness labeled schizophrenia, the first report on mental health was issued by David Satcher, former Surgeon General of the United States (USDHHS, 1999). In part, this report sought to replace earlier folk beliefs and misinformation about mental illness with scientific knowledge. Prior to that time, no surgeon general had focused the time, federal resources, and personal energy on helping the nation to understand severe mental illness, its probable causes, and approaches to effective treatments by examining its scientific basis. No other surgeon general in history had conceptualized a relationship between the status of the mentally ill and the overall health and well-being of the nation. Although a small number of federal agencies had published reports that addressed various aspects of severe mental illness, previous surgeons general had assiduously avoided this area and the policy implications for the nation in the past. The focus in prior years had been on more traditional physical illnesses or communicable diseases.

A year later, Satcher issued the first ever report that linked race, ethnicity, and culture to both mental illness and psychiatric care (USDHHS, 2001). Both of these reports sought to respond to the current dilemmas and confusion surrounding the conceptual and operational definitions of mental illness, theories of causation, and scientifically supported treatments of severe mental illness. However, Satcher's second report, of necessity, had to identify, address, and correct many of the putative linkages between these illnesses and a plethora of social, cultural, and racial factors that had been falsely and poorly addressed throughout the history of psychiatry and mental health policy in the United States (Babcock, 1895; Cartwright, 1851; Conrad, 1871; Malzberg, 1953, 1959; Parker and Kleiner, 1966; Pasamanick, 1963a). Were blacks truly more at risk of severe mental illness than whites, as had been cited in the literature for decades? Were the clinical treatment methods that were effective with white populations appropriate for blacks? Did black populations seek psychiatric help in the same patterns as did their white fellow citizens? Or were the discrepancies in frequency of illness rates a reflection of misdiagnosis or the application of inappropriate research methodologies (Fischer, 1969; Jackson et al., 1996; Neighbors and Jackson, 1996)? The correlations between a variety of sociocultural factors and severe mental illness were heretofore addressed in the research literature with excessive subjectiveness and bias. The racial bias was so pervasive that Quincy Jones and his family could not have obtained much clarity about the extent to which race, culture, or ethnicity influences either the onset of such illnesses or their resolution. The findings and recommendations in Satcher's two reports seek to address many of these long-term conceptual and practical dilemmas and underscore the importance of the history of mental health care for African Americans in the United States. However, the report places less focus on the need for an exploration of current and future public policy linking race, culture, ethnicity, and mental illness. The absence of an extensive focus on policy is the major weakness in the report.

This chapter will identify and examine the historical concepts, research, data, ideas, services, and policy approaches that formed the earliest ideological basis of mental health services to African-American populations. These approaches reflect an admixture of scientific hypotheses about severe mental illness as well as the racial views held about African-American citizens in the United States. Public policies often ran parallel to this admixture of science and racism. In the second portion of the chapter, the focus will be on developing a summary of the specific elements included in the former surgeon general's report that are useful in dispelling and countering the panoply of earlier unscientific notions about the relationship between racial vulnerability and severe mental illness. The chapter concludes with an identification of some future public policy implications and direction for mental health care for African-American populations.

RACE AND MENTAL ILLNESS IN HISTORICAL PERSPECTIVE: 1763-1963

The history of public policies and services for the severely mentally ill reveals that for close to 2,000 years, societies throughout the world have had limited understanding or even tolerance for severe mental illness and the mentally ill (Dain, 1964; Focault, 1965; Greenblatt et al., 1955; Rothman, 1970; Torrey, 1988). These societies have also struggled at times to create a range of humane public policies to treat the mentally ill population while also protecting their civil and human rights and simultaneously those of the general public. At times, persons with mental illness were considered so dangerous to the public that their rights to free access were severely curtailed. The stigma and fear associated with severe mental illness has influenced the public to clamor for policies that ease the transition of individuals with mental illness into state institutions, based on the beliefs that these individuals represent a danger to the public. In most instances, elected officials complied with these public fears by crafting policies that tended to maintain mentally ill individuals in institutions for life. Other societies crafted their policies on a unitary hypothesis of mental illness and a singular treatment strategy (institutionalization), although it seems increasingly evident that serious mental illnesses are multiple brain diseases with multiple causes requiring multiple policy solutions (Andreasen, 1984; Gottesman and Shields, 1998; Kendler and Diehl, 1993; Kety, 1987).

Historically, most government policies and societal responses to severe mental illness can be categorized into five cyclical and overlapping periods: community neglect (pre-1700); institutionalization (1763-1963); deinstitutionalization (1963-1980); community mental health (1963-1993); and managed behavioral health care (post-1993). Of the five cyclical periods of policy development, institutionalization, principally through state government policy and funding, was by far the most extensive—chronologically, psychologically, educationally, and financially. The utilization of state hospitals raised the most significant ethical, political, clinical, fiscal, and legal questions for all levels of government throughout history, although the federal government avoided direct responsibility for decades (Davis, 1998; Ennis and Siegel, 1973).

The utilization of the mental institution as an all-purpose almshouse was a worldwide phenomena. The history of the psychiatric asylum extends from the opening of the first institution in Baghdad in 750 A.D. to the opening of the new psychiatric institute in Missouri in 2001. Historically, in the United States, state governments have had primary responsibility for promulgating complex public mental health policies that determined admission criteria, standards of treatment, and the circumstances required for discharge and readmission to state hospitals. States also exercised the right to determine policies on who paid for psychiatric care until the development of federal Medicaid and Medicare regulations in 1963.

Two of the most complex questions that faced state legislative bodies centered on the relationship between race and the vulnerability to mental illness and the right to access treatment by race. Similar questions were raised about the relationship between property ownership and vulnerability to mental illness. Because of the assumed relationship between wealth, ownership, citizenship, and rights, the founders of the United States extended this logic to vulnerability to disease. Early in the history of the colonies, state governments were uncertain whether enslaved Africans were more or less susceptible to severe forms of mental illness than whites, or whose responsibility it was to ensure that this population received care. If in fact slaves were vulnerable to mental disorder, was it the responsibility of the government or of their owners to procure services for them? Scientists offered little help to policymakers since they too were uncertain about the psychic apparatus of people in bondage. There were fewer questions raised about freeborn Africans who had American citizenship, and were permitted access to state hospital care, albeit separate and unequally from that provided to whites (Drewry, 1916). Freeborn Africans could access mental health care in state institutions under state policies, as long as they did not displace whites, equally in need of psychiatric services. The relationship between race and the need for specialized services for Africans, separate from those for whites, was raised in the first meeting of state hospital superintendents held in 1844 (Drewry, 1916). The superintendents concluded, after considerable debate, that services for insane colored people were inadequate, particularly in the southern states. However, it remained unclear whether the position proposed that southern state governments should be required to provide services for this population or whether such responsibility should rest with the slave owner. There was also the question of whether the state or the owner carried any responsibility for securing mental health care for slaves. The policy position of the southern states was even more difficult and tenuous because of the pressure to maintain an economy based on chattel slave labor. Open access to potentially long-term psychiatric hospitalization might undermine the economy. To enhance the quality and access to inpatient mental health care for enslaved and freeborn Africans, the superintendents established a committee of their members and asked them to develop a draft of a national policy that could be adopted and applied by individual state governments. However, the question of the vulnerability of Africans to mental illness remained unanswered, at least directly, and the question of the relationship between their enslaved status and mental health risk, were not openly discussed.

The Commonwealth of Virginia was the first state to develop mental health policies and inpatient hospital services generally for the severely mentally ill, as well as those that specifically governed African Americans (Drewry, 1916; Hurd et al., 1916). Initially, a limited number of freeborn Africans were allowed access to the state hospital at Williamsburg between 1763 and 1840. However, after 1840 the Virginia government became concerned about the increasing unmet psychiatric needs of enslaved Africans and the pressure that their need for care exerted on existing institutions. Coupled with this concern was the concern that the two racial populations should not mix within a single facility. These concerns stimulated consideration in Virginia for alternative institutions that would provide psychiatric services for slaves and free blacks, separate from those of whites. It was thus not unexpected that Virginia resolved its racial policy dilemma by becoming the first state to establish a system of hospital-based care, segregated by race from 1869 to 1968, or that Virginia became one of the last states to yield to new federal policy directions mandating integrated mental health and education (Hurd et al., 1916).

THE QUANTIFICATION OF PSYCHIATRIC MISERY

Research on the potential correlations between race and mental illness has focused principally on questions and hypotheses related to morbidity, prevalence, incidence, and more recently issues of consumption patterns. However, the research literature has largely ignored wide areas of investigation around questions of the impact of race on public policy development, the burden of mental illness on black families, or the extent to which African Americans participate in mental health advocacy and policy formulation. To date there have not been any major policy studies reported in the literature that focus on either the evolution of such policies, analysis of their content, or the impact of key mental health policies on African Americans (Davis, 2001). Nor has there been any consistent effort to collect, catalog, and maintain significant documents of archival significance on the black experience in mental health care circa 1868-1965 (Davis, 1998).

One of the earliest references to the relationship between race and mental illness found in the literature is the United States Census of 1840. This was the first census that identified the number of persons in institutions. However, this federal document reached an erroneous conclusion that there was a significant difference in the frequency of mental illness by race and region of the country in which a black person lived and by citizenship. Enslaved blacks who lived in the South purportedly had considerably lower rates of mental illness than free blacks in northern states. Methodologically, the 1840 census on persons in institutions relied on data drawn from admissions to public mental hospitals. However, at the time the census was completed few public hospitals in northern states admitted blacks as patients. There were no hospitals for blacks exclusively in the South, and only one hospital in the United States admitted both free blacks and whites (Drewry, 1916; Thomas and Sillen, 1972). Although there were serious methodological flaws in the way that census data was collected and presented, Jarvis (1844) utilized these figures as scientific evidence of significant differences in the risk of mental illness by race. It was not until 1852 that Jarvis retracted his earlier statements and confirmed that the data were biased by an interest in maintaining bondage.

The census materials provided a quantitative basis for the continuation of Southern ideology and practices of slavery. However, perhaps inadvertently, the census data also supported the perceptions and petition of state hospital superintendents throughout the country (Drewry, 1916). The superintendents indicated that mentally ill blacks, whether slave or free, were not obtaining adequate care in state mental hospitals. According to the superintendents, the problem of uneven or total absence of access to hospital care was more pronounced in the southern states. However, there appeared to be little difference between the degree of access to state hospitals by race or region. Blacks with mental illness were denied access to state hospitals in both northern and southern states with almost equal frequency. The exception to the status quo was the practice in Virginia of admitting freeborn blacks to Eastern State Hospital while maintaining segregation by race.

Controversy over the 1840 census may have also helped influence the passage of legislation in Virginia that allowed enslaved Africans access to the state hospital at Williamsburg. Three conditions, however, were required in the legislation that circumscribed access by race: No enslaved Africans could be admitted without a petition from their owner or person who held jurisdiction over them. This first requirement was influenced greatly by the second policy requirement that the petitioner had to pay for the inpatient care of the enslaved African. The third requirement of this early policy in Virginia would not allow the admission of an enslaved African to reduce admission or treatment opportunities for whites. No reference or mention is made in the policy about the potential impact on the admission and treatment opportunities for free blacks of this change in policy (Table 6.1).

During the 1844 meeting of the Association of State Hospital Superintendents and Physicians, the Association appointed a three-person committee (two members were from Virginia) to create a national policy for the association on the need for care of insane colored persons. The debate stimulated by the statistical conclusions reached in the 1840 census appears to have produced three very important policy changes in Virginia. In 1845, the superintendent of Western State

TABLE 6.1. Chronological Development of Mental Health Policies

Year	Direction and Content of Public Policy
1700	Local mental health acts create local responsibility for the mentally ill.
1763	Virginia creates the first state-supported mental hospital.
1774	Virginia permits freeborn Africans admission to state hospital, but care is segregated by race.
1800	84 percent of states develop mental hospitals at state expense.
1846	Virginia permits enslaved Africans admission, but whites retain first priority for services.
1847	Virginia legislature considers the feasibility of building a separate hospital for colored mentally ill.
1853	President Pierce vetoes law allowing federal support of state mental hospitals.
1869	Virginia creates first hospital in the United States exclusively for colored insane.
1870	Other southern states adopt Virginia legislation and create separate places.
1875	North Carolina passes similar legislation.
1910	Alabama creates a separate mental institution for colored.
1912	Maryland creates a separate mental institution for colored.
1930	United States establishes division of mental health in public health service.
1942	American men unable to pass physical exams for military service.
1946	Congress creates single state mental health agencies and NIMH.
1955	Congress creates first presidential commission on mental illness.
1963	Congress passes Kennedy's community mental health bill.

Hospital recommended to the Virginia General Assembly that consideration be given to the establishment of a separate hospital for insane blacks (Hurd et al., 1916).

Then in 1846 the Virginia General Assembly gave the superintendent of Eastern State Hospital permission to admit enslaved Africans for treatment. The Virginia General Assembly passed a resolution in

1848 that permitted both of its state hospitals to develop a plan for either expanding their facilities to accommodate enslaved Africans with mental illness or plans for constructing a separate facility.

Despite these policy developments in Virginia and the effort by Jarvis to refute the data used in the 1840 census, physicians and learned medical societies continued to use the biased data to support arguments that blacks, who were once considered immune from mental illness, were mentally inferior to whites and that freedom increased their psychiatric risk. In 1851, Cartwright published findings to conclude that enslaved Africans were at less risk of mental illness than those who were either born free or had acquired their freedom and moved to northern states (Cartwright, 1851).

John Galt, the first superintendent of a state hospital, added to the confused logic regarding linkages between psychiatric risk and race. In one instance Galt appeared to take a significant leadership position in advocating equitable services without regard to race or citizenship. However, Galt then put forth the argument that enslaved Africans were relatively immune from mental illness because slaves were virtually free of the stresses that stem from the ownership of property and related assets. Galt indicated that because of their property-less class, enslaved Africans were considered less at risk than their white owners who held and managed property. Galt also proposed to the Virginia legislature that enslaved Africans would become more vulnerable to mental illness and would need additional inpatient care if and when slavery ended. Because of his stature, the conclusions reached and shared by Galt had the potential to influence both mental health practice and public policy for a number of years.

Although Edward Jarvis published a refutation in 1852 of his earlier findings and conclusions, newspapers and scientific journals continued to use this data to support the continuation of slavery and resistance to reconstruction (Andrews, 1887; Babcock, 1895). Between 1900 and 1963 a vast literature developed in scientific journals that continued the debate over psychiatric risk, frequency, service utilization, and race. However, the tone and direction in the scientific literature changed markedly in the 1960s as the civil rights struggle increased in power and urban confrontations started (Fischer, 1969). In the 1960s public opinion and public policy reflected the premise that African Americans were highly at risk because of urban environments, stress, and migration (Faris and Dunham, 1939; Malzberg and

Lee, 1956; O'Malley, 1914; Parker and Kleiner, 1966; Pasamanick et al., 1960; Riessman, Cohn, and Pearl, 1964; Rose, 1955).

Rothman's (1970) book is viewed as one of the more comprehensive reviews of the historical development of social thought about mental illness and the rise of mental institutions. Rothman traces the parallel development of beliefs, fears, ideas, and attitudes toward the mentally ill and the development of key public policies that created large state hospitals. He makes a clear and compelling case for the relationship between emerging public policy in mental health and the perception by the public of the impact of persons with mental illness on the overall stability of society. The more risk there is for society as a whole, the greater the extent to which societal policies stress institutionalization, according to Rothman. Although Rothman addresses the development of mental illness and services in the European and Native American populations, he does not address similar issues related to enslaved or free African Americans, although this population was seen from 1840 forward as at greater risk. Dain's (1964) work chronicles the history and development of the first state mental institution in the United States for the mentally ill. However, this work does not focus on issues related to race and mental health care. Thomas and Sillen's (1972) book does examine in considerable depth the history of mental health care extended to African Americans and the influence of racism on the psychiatric profession and to some extent on public policy. Morais' (1967) book on race and medicine provides an excellent review of both health and mental health issues and their linkage to policies and race.

PREVALENCE AND INCIDENCE OF MENTAL ILLNESS BY RACE

Overall, the research literature reflects two diametrically opposing views on prevalence and incidence of mental illness by race. These two positions have greatly influenced the development of policies and services for African Americans and may help explain many of the dilemmas found by the former surgeon general. In one period of history (1800-1869), African Americans were viewed as having an immunity to severe mental illness, while in another (1869-1963), African Americans were described as being highly at risk of severe mental illness either because of their inability to manage freedom or life in the city. In the period 1800-1869, the absence of psychiatric vulnerability supported public policies at the state government level that generally denied enslaved blacks access to mental health care. However, in the latter period (1869-1963), the perception of risk by race supported policies that increased hospitalization far beyond expected frequencies. What is clear from the review of the literature is that there has historically been a significant gap in knowledge about the relationship between the evolution and content of public policies and services and the prevailing racial perspectives held in the society.

A series of historical studies of the health status of American populations concluded that there were very significant differences in prevalence and incidence of physical and mental health problems between groups based on color, income, and residence. However, the majority of these studies have been based on admissions by race to public psychiatric hospitals and have not controlled for income nor the difference between admission to a state hospital and the actual presence of severe mental illness (Jackson et al., 1996; Neighbors, 1994; Neighbors et al., 1989; Reiger et al., 1993; Snowden, 1982; Willie, Kramer, and Brown, 1973). It has been only recently that these studies and their conclusions have been challenged as having faulty methodology.

It has been noted that people of color, particularly residents of inner cities, demonstrate major disparities in their health status when compared to other populations (Center for Health Economics Research, 1993; Robert Wood Johnson Foundation, 1991). The disparities noted in the literature cover the range of disorders from high neonatal mortality rates per live birth, higher rates of heart and circulatory problems, disproportionate rates of AIDS and related deaths, greater prevalence of chronic conditions, higher rates of edentulism, and higher rates of admissions to psychiatric facilities (Center for Health Economics Research, 1993; Robert Wood Johnson Foundation, 1991). The high incidence of substance abuse, physical injuries, and deaths from violence greatly distinguish low-income black neighborhoods and communities in terms of potential and actual costs of health care. According to some reports, substance abuse is the most significant health problem in the nation (Institute for Health Policy, 1993). These populations also show lower availability of health insurance and a significantly lower proportion of health professionals within easy access of their neighborhoods. The gap in mental health policy research is more pronounced in relationship to the earliest policies that established and maintained segregated systems of mental health services prior to 1900, principally in southern states. Our understanding of the societal factors that precipitated key, and oftentimes contradictory, policies is very limited (McCandless, 1996; Rothman, 1970). Over several decades, research and public attention have been focused primarily on the questions of morbidity of severe mental illness and the rates of consumption of services (particularly inpatient) by race (Babcock, 1895; Cartwright, 1851; Dain, 1964; Deutsch, 1944; Evarts, 1914; Fischer, 1969; Jarvis, 1844; Malzberg, 1963; Manderscheid and Sonnenschein, 1987; Neighbors and Lumpkin, 1990; Pasamanick, 1963b; Witmer, 1891). While the data on prevalence, incidence, and service utilization was considered critical up through the 1960s, there remained a need to focus more specific efforts on the interpretation and integration of these data and the resulting social policy questions related to African-American experiences in the mental health system: Why did the Commonwealth of Virginia provide mental health care to freeborn blacks prior to 1800, but deny that same care to enslaved Africans until 1844? Why did the Commonwealth of Virginia reverse its policy of partially integrated care in 1869 and develop separate mental institutions by race, but make no distinctions by former slave status? What was the impact of the implementation of deinstitutionalization policy in the 1960s on African Americans with mental illness? What was the impact of community mental health policy and services on African Americans with mental illness? These are important policy questions that must be studied and examined further.

HISTORIC PATTERNS OF UTILIZATION OF MENTAL HEALTH SERVICE BY RACE

The major public policy paradoxes that are identified in the report of the former surgeon general have been raised and debated in the United States since the early 1700s (Jarvis, 1852) (Table 6.2). The first of these paradoxes centered on the incidence and prevalence of severe mental illness in populations of African ancestry, while the second centered on the extent to which these populations require and consume public and/or proprietary mental health services (Snowden and Cheung, 1990).

TABLE 6.2. Phases of Mental Health Ideology and Public Policy by Year

Period	Service, Research, and Racial Perspective Held in Society
1763-1844	Africans were considered immune from the development of mental disorders because only persons who owned property were considered at risk; freeborn blacks were provided access; rates of mental illness were considered low.
1845-1863	Freedom and citizenship were considered harmful to the mental health status of slaves; Africans considered intellectually and morally inferior to whites; predictions that rates of illness would rise with freedom; more hospitals needed.
1864-1963	Negroes were considered as highly vulnerable to mental illness and mental retardation; separate state facilities established; admission of Negroes to state facilities increased significantly.
1964-1980	Migration from rural southern states to urban cities in the North is hypothesized to increase the risk of mental illness; admissions to mental hospitals exceeds rates for all other American populations; limited services from community mental health centers established under Kennedy.
1981-1998	Several studies show no significant difference exists in risk, vulnerability, or rates by race or ethnicity; disproportionate admissions are related to societal beliefs, poverty, and social policy; admission rates of blacks exceed expected frequency; African Americans overconsume inpatient services; high rates of misdiagnosis; participation in mental health advocacy is low.

Historically, the answers to these two interrelated sets of public policy paradoxes concerning race and mental illness have been more a reflection of the prevailing racial climate in American society at large than with objective epidemiological or ethnographic data. A cursory review of the data on admissions to inpatient psychiatric facilities shows disproportionately high rates of admissions by race to all types of facilities (Jackson, Neighbors, and Gurin, 1986; Manderscheid and Sonnenschein, 1987; Scheffler, 1991; Snowden and Cheung, 1990). Some of this data (Manderscheid and Sonnenschein, 1987) consistently shows that between 1980 and 1992, the rate of admission for all persons to state hospitals in the United States was approximately 163.6 per 100,000. The rate for whites was 136, while the rate for Hispanics was 146 and the rate for Native Americans and Asians was 142 per 100,000. The admission rate to state hospitals for consumers of African ancestry for that same year was 364.2 per 100,000 population.

When admission to private psychiatric hospitals is considered by race, it is noted that the rate for all persons was 62.6 per 100,000, while the rate for whites was slightly above the mean at 63.4. The rate of admissions to private psychiatric hospitals for Hispanics was 34.4, while the rate for Native Americans and Asians was 29.6. The rate for persons of African ancestry was close to the national mean at 62.9.

Admissions to general hospitals with psychiatric units showed similar patterns by race and ethnicity. For the population as a whole the rate was 295.3 per 100,000, while the rate for the white population as a whole was 284.9. The rate of admissions for Hispanics was 227 and the rate for Native Americans and Asians was 221.7. The rate during the same period for persons of African ancestry admitted to general hospital psychiatric units was 386.6 per 100,000.

While the national mean admission rate to Veterans' Administration Hospitals was 70.4 per 100,000, populations of African ancestry had a rate of 118.2 per 100,000. No other racial or ethnic population had an admission rate to the Veterans' Administration Hospitals that approximated the rate for populations of African ancestry.

When age is examined, the relationship between admissions to psychiatric hospitals and race is more pronounced. For example, the rate of admissions to state psychiatric hospitals for consumers of African ancestry between the ages of eighteen and twenty-four was 598 per 100,000 while the national mean was 163.6. The most excessive rate found was for consumers of African ancestry between the ages of twenty-five and forty-four where 753 per 100,000 were admitted to state psychiatric hospitals. Although admissions are not indicative of actual prevalence rates in the population, what is clearly shown is an inveterate pattern of service utilization differentiated by race and class (Manderscheid and Sonnenschein, 1987).

To a great extent, access to and consumption of psychiatric inpatient services by consumers of African ancestry has historically paralleled the prevailing theoretical views of their vulnerability and morbidity and the extent to which diagnoses are culturally competent. During the colonial era, when blacks were believed to be less susceptible to mental disorder, public policies extended inpatient services to free blacks but denied similar services to enslaved blacks until 1844. Given the numerical imbalance between free and enslaved blacks at that time, the low utilization of existing services by those enslaved supported the hypothesis of lower susceptibility. The more recent idea that blacks were more vulnerable to major mental disorders parallels the socioeconomic and political conflicts surrounding the abolition of slavery and pressure for reconstruction. By 1863, separate mental institutions were created for blacks throughout the southern and border states (Hurd et al., 1916). As freedom for blacks drew closer, it was predicted that there would be a need for a major increase in mental hospital beds to accommodate those who would suffer from post slavery stress disorder. Data from the 1840 census was used to show that the frequency of mental illness was eleven times higher for free northern blacks than for those in bondage in the South (Thomas and Sillen, 1972). Similar data was used to show that the ratio of serious mental illness in southern blacks was considerably less than the ratio in southern whites, while the reverse was found in northern states.

The mental illness perspective between 1945 and 1985 was that black and other urban populations were far more susceptible to major mental illness because of a greater frequency of poverty, life stress, and migration to urban areas (Faris and Dunham, 1939; Hollingshead and Redlich, 1958; Kramer, Rosen, and Willis, 1973; Locke, Kramer, and Pasamanick, 1960). It was this data and its conclusions that President Kennedy used to base a portion of his successful legislative rationale for the establishment of community mental health centers in 1963. The prevailing belief in the 1960s that urban blacks were more vulnerable to mental illness resulted in policies that facilitated excess involuntary admissions from 1863 to the 1990s (Jones and Gray, 1986; Ramm, 1989). During this time, the number of blacks admitted to various psychiatric institutions grew at a disproportionate rate, with a sizeable number admitted involuntarily.

Data from the 1960s through the 1980s showed that African Americans were more frequently diagnosed on admission with severe mental illness than other ethnic or racial populations (Manderscheid and Sonnenschein, 1987). Admissions of African Americans to state mental hospitals showed that 56 percent of these individuals received a primary diagnosis of schizophrenia, while only 38 percent of all individuals admitted received a similar diagnosis. Hispanics too received a disproportionately high (44 percent) rate of severe mental illness diagnoses on admission to state mental institutions (Flaskerud and Hu, 1992; Garretson, 1993; Jones and Gray, 1986; Lawson et al., 1994), leading to the conclusion that the primary reason for the disproportionate rate of severe mental illness diagnoses are errors made by diagnosticians who are unfamiliar with mental illness as it is manifested in populations of color. It is this questionable data and misleading information that forms the basis, at least in part, of the need for a comprehensive review, assessment, and guidance by the Surgeon General of the United States.

THE SURGEON GENERAL'S REPORT 2001: CORRECTING THE PAST, CHARTING THE FUTURE

Although the purpose of the 1999 and 2001 reports was not ostensibly to correct past scientific, political, or policy errors, these reports indirectly had to offset years of incorrect data and assumptions about race and mental illness. Data and information errors range from faulty definitions of key terms to statistical data on the frequency of mental disorders in populations by race and ethnicity. Although the surgeon general's office or task force did not actually gather and analyze new data, three data and information strategies were important: (1) definitions of key terms and concepts, (2) review of current literature on prevalence and incidence in the target populations, and (3) presentation of findings from current studies on causation and treatment outcomes.

Definitions

Over many decades, a clear and fairly universal definition of mental health has been illusive at best. The first report by the former surgeon general proposed that mental illness be best viewed as a "term that refers collectively to all diagnosable mental disorders" (USDHHS, 1999, p. 4). These disorders, on the other hand, are described as health conditions, eliminating the mind-body dualism that for so long separated mental health from other health problems. Mental disorders share in common a number of characteristics: "alterations in thinking, mood, or behavior associated with distress, and/or impaired functioning" (p. 4). The range of disorders that then fall into this category include Alzheimer's disease, major depression, obsessive-compulsive disorder, bipolar disorder, and schizophrenia. Of these mental disorders, schizophrenia is considered the most debilitating or disabling. However, the former surgeon general notes that when compared to other health problems, mental disorders rank very high as a source of burden.

For much of the twentieth century the conceptualization of mental illness generally, and severe mental illness specifically, was influenced by the psychoanalytically based theoretical perspectives of Adler, Freud, Janet, Jung, and Meyers, as well as the clinical description by Kraeplin (Sadler, 1936). In one of the more influential psychiatric texts, Sadler (1936) suggested that early in the twentieth century the emerging field of psychiatry defined severe mental illness, particularly psychosis, as "a breakdown of the ego—a flight from adult adjustment back to the fantasy of childhood" (p. 779). These earlier views made an effort to distinguish severe mental illness or insanity from psychoneurosis, whose origins and prognosis were considered of substantial different quality and unrelated to psychosis. Sadler and others did not conceptualize a continuum in psychiatric disorders that linked psychoneurosis and psychosis but did ascribe similar risks associated with hereditary vulnerability. Sadler concluded that severe mental illness could be seen as a threat to the order and stability of society, and he predicted that such disorders would become "one of the major problems of modern society" (p. 779). Sadler's view of mental illness as a societal threat is captured too in the writings of Rothman (1970). However, Rothman proposes that the sense of threat and impending instability within seventeenth century America had its origins in a host of behaviors, from poverty to criminality, for which institutionalization was proposed as the ideal solution. Rothman proposed that the central role of the institution became transfixed in American public policy; an obsession that continues to the present.

Sadler concluded that the causes of severe mental illness ranged from purely genetic predisposition to environmental antecedents, social environment, and race (1936). However, much of their treatment philosophy and conceptualization of these disorders centered around traditional psychoanalytic concepts and treatment constructs that tended to dismiss pursuit of other variables. The narrowness of these concepts too may have delayed scientific consideration and examination of other pertinent variables. Over the century, vulnerability and risk of severe mental illness was attributed more to the quality and nature of interaction between the child and parents (Bateson et al.,

1956; Jackson, 1960). It was out of the theoretical musings of Bateson and Jackson that the behavior of mothers was ascribed a causative variable in the onset of severe mental illness.

Because of the theoretical perspective held on prognosis and the treatment of severe mental illness, most earlier public policies required that the person be hospitalized in a state mental institution and separated from the offending environment and family believed to either cause or exacerbate the illness.

Prevalence and Incidence Rates

The Surgeon General's Report relies on data from a series of studies conducted between 1984 to 1998 to reach new conclusions about race and mental health. The major finding from these studies is that, contrary to earlier assumptions, there is no significant difference in rates of mental illness by race or ethnicity in the United States (Kessler et al., 1994; Regier et al., 1993; Robins and Regier, 1991) (Table 6.3). What does differ by race and ethnicity is diagnosis, help-seeking, access to services, utilization of mental health services, and participation in research studies (Neighbors et al., 1989; Segal, Bola, and Watson, 1996; Snowden and Cheung, 1990; Takeuchi and Cheung, 1998; Takeuchi, Sue, and Yeh, 1995; Takeuchi and Uehara, 1996).

Summary of Report

The Surgeon General's Report focuses on four target populations: African Americans, Native Americans and Alaskan Natives, Asian Americans and Pacific Islanders, and Hispanic Americans (Table 6.4). The report relies on an extensive review of the research literature to reach its conclusions about people of color, including children, adolescents, adults, and the aged. In almost all of the groups surveyed the least amount of information was available about children and the aging population.

POLICY IMPLICATIONS

The two reports from the former surgeon general offer a rare series of challenges to the established mental health system in both the private and public sectors. In some respects these reports are reminis-

TABLE 6.3. Results of the ECA and NCS Studies of Mental Health Care for African Americans

	ECA			NCS		
	Black	**White**	**Total**	**Black**	**White**	**Total**
	n = 4,638	n = 12,944	n = 19,182	n = 666	n = 4,498	n = 5,877
	% (se)	% (se)	% (se)	% (se)	% (se)	% (se)
12-month						
Major Depression	2.2 (0.1)	2.8 (0.6)	2.7	8.2 (1.1)	9.9 (0.6)	10.0 (0.6)
Panic Disorder	1.0 (0.3)	0.9 (0.1)	0.9 (0.1)	1.1 (0.5)	2.4 (0.3)	2.2 (0.2)
Phobic Disorder	16.2 (1.5)	9.1 (0.4)	9.7 (0.4)	14.5 (1.8)	14.8 (0.6)	15.0 (0.6)
Lifetime						
Major Depression	3.1	5.1	4.9	1.6 (1.4)	17.7 (0.7)	16.9 (0.6)
Dysthymia	4.0	6.3	3.2	5.4 (1.0)	6.7 (0.4)	6.5 (0.4)
Panic Disorder	1.3 (0.4)	1.6 (0.1)	1.6 (0.1)	1.4 (0.5)	3.9 (0.3)	3.4 (0.2)
Phobic Disorder	23.4 (0.5)	9.7 (3.2)	14.3 (0.4)	9.2 (2.0)	22.3 (0.8)	21.9 (0.7)

Source: Snowden (2001)
The SE (Standard Error) is the average dispersion concerning the percentage.

cent of the President's Commission on Mental Health in 1955 and its report (Joint Commission on Mental Health, 1961) that helped change public mental health systems. The reports also present challenges to universities and colleges, professional educational programs, voluntary associations, mental health professional associations, and consumers and families in racial and ethnic communities. Each of these sectors has helped maintain the current system, in spite of data and information that suggest a different path. The content of these reports should foster questions anew about what has heretofore passed for acceptable scientific knowledge about race, ethnicity, culture, and mental health and illness.

The reports offer the nation a compilation of studies and findings that basically counter centuries of folk wisdom, misinformation, disinformation, and outright falsehoods about race, mental health, and illness. Most of the studies included in the report challenge hypotheses formulated in the nineteenth century that linked increased risk,

TABLE 6.4. Summary of Key Findings by Ethnic Group in the Surgeon General's Report

	Selected Findings	Conclusions
African Americans	Low rates of depression	1. Rates similar to national rates for other populations
	Higher female depression	
	Higher frequency of phobias	2. Culture is significant to treatment outcomes
	Poverty linked to illness rate	
	Sparse info on children	3. Use of alternative services is increasing
	Sparse info on aged	4. Income is related to rate of mental illness and service utilization
	High rates of somatization	
	Low suicide rates	
	High rates of homelessness	5. Sparse number of African-American providers
	High use of inpatient service	6. Low access to services
		7. Increased risk of misdiagnosis
		8. Not included in key research studies
		9. Key disparities remain
Native Americans	High rates of PTSD in military veterans	1. Data on rates and service usage is limited
	80 percent higher substance abuse	2. Need for service appears higher than average
	SA determines service usage	3. High comorbidity between mental illness and SA
	Poverty unrelated to illness	4. Limited information on help-seeking patterns
	SA rates high in adolescence	
	High rate of aged depression	5. Some changes in policy are noted
	High rate of AHADD	6. Limited outcome info
	Highest suicide rates	7. Traditional healing is important
	High rate of conduct disorder	8. Need to consider strengths perspective
	High use of inpatient service	
		9. Key disparities remain

Asian Americans	Moderate rate of depression	1. Info on population and mental health is limited
	DSM-IV not as relevant	
	Culture-bound syndromes	2. Rates are similar to those of other populations
	Few Asians in study samples	
	Sparse info on children	3. Increased need for culture-based services
	Sparse info on aged	4. Population may underconsume services
	Mind/body integration	
	Lowest suicide rates	5. Help-seeking pattern marked by delay
	Low substance abuse rate	
	Low inpatient use	6. Stigma is high
	Language and refugee issues	7. More research is needed on population use and needs
		8. Cultural-bound syndromes are important focus
		9. Key disparities remain
Hispanic Americans	High PTSD in military veterans	1. Traditional mental health system fails
	Depression in adolescents	2. Risks for youth are higher than all
	Rates linked to origin	
	U.S.-born higher rates	3. U.S. birth and life is related to greater risk
	Children at high risk	
	Depression in aged	4. Rates seen as similar to whites
	Low substance abuse	
	Low suicide rates	5. Key strengths in culture and history
	Low homelessness	6. Key disparities remain
	Moderate inpatient	
	Language issues	

vulnerability, and admissions to public mental institutions to race, ethnicity, and non-European cultural backgrounds. In some instances, these hypotheses proposed varying levels of vulnerability based on the prevailing political dynamics, rather than valid psychiatric sequelae. The studies indirectly conclude that the disproportionate frequency of severe mental illness in people of color was the likely artifact of clinical and training protocols influenced by long-standing societal beliefs about racial inferiority and worth. This diagnosis and treatment based on societal belief systems often resulted in major errors in diagnosis, not only in mental health but in primary care and specialty health care. However, old ideas and perspectives, even when wrong and harmful, can be terribly resistant to change, as evident by Jarvis' effort to rescind his misinterpretation of data on mental illness and race drawn from the 1840 census. In a society that felt it was losing its moorings, Jarvis' unscientific notions that stability could be enhanced through control of deviant classes found enthusiastic support in public policies that created and sustained omnibus institutions. That women, Asians, Mexicans, or the poor became the major residents and inmates of these institutions over time seemed fitting, given the convoluted logic of public policy around matters of race and poverty. Between 1840 and 2002, thousands of people of color in the United States have been unable to obtain the level of mental health services that they needed, while simultaneously being exposed to the most restrictive level of services that were unnecessary and clinically unwarranted in most cases.

The most critical implication of the former surgeon general's two reports is to determine how this knowledge of what works and what needs to be done finds its way into the public discourse, state plans, and federal strategy. It is unclear whether the federal government will take responsibility for ensuring that there are changes made within state mental health systems that are consistent with these findings? How will the findings impact managed health care plans? Will the federal government offer new funding to state and local governments to support services? Will state governments accept collaborative relations with the federal government around mental health planning and policy development? Does the Bush administration have a strategic plan in mind for implementing the recommendations included in the report throughout federal mental health organizations and policies?

African-American social workers are strategically positioned to serve as advocates and organizers in the mental health arena, but this has not occurred to the extent that is necessary to change long-term entrenched social policy and precedents. In fact, the presence of social workers on the front line of policy change in mental health has declined, parallel with the rise of managed behavioral health care. To alter this circumstance, there must be renewed opportunities to educate social workers and communities about the new research and findings on mental health and illness of people of African ancestry and other oppressed populations represented in the surgeon general's report. This report can be used as a major tool to both educate and motivate groups toward policy change and advocacy.

Second, social work and mental health organizations, particularly those of African ancestry, need to organize coalitions of consumers, family members, providers, researchers, and educators who can collectively lobby for increased access, culturally competent services, and community-based mental health care that meets the needs of the population. Such coalitions allow for more diverse voices and a greater number of constituent groups to address calcified policies.

Third, African-American social workers must be prepared to create and manage community-based mental health services that are culturally competent and rooted in the needs of the community. This means that there needs to be more advanced training for social workers in mental health services, culturally competent service delivery, and management of non-profit organizations.

Fourth, African-American social workers should educate communities on mental health and provide more understanding of what is required for recovery and rehabilitation. Connecting individuals and families to treatment and providing referrals could be an additional function of this community mental health education campaign. However, the primary focus should rest on developing culturally competent educational tools and media campaigns that can better educate communities of African ancestry about mental health and mental illness and the central role of public policy.

CONCLUSION

Although the former surgeon general's name is on these two groundbreaking reports, they really have been written by hundreds of other government officials and private citizens who have remained in place after his disengagement from office. One general policy question here is whether citizens and bureaucrats will build on the challenges presented in the reports to alter and replace ineffective policies. However, the issue that will determine whether the disparities noted in the Surgeon General's Report will remain or be addressed in public policy is whether African-American social workers assume a key advocacy role in dismantling the historical myths of mental illness and lobbying for greater access and a better quality of services.

REFERENCES

Andreasen, N. C. (1984). *The broken brain.* New York: Harper and Row.

Andrews, J. B. (1887). The distribution and care of the insane in the United States. *Transactions of the International Medical Congress, Ninth Session.*

Babcock, J. W. (1895). The colored insane. *Alienist and Neurologist, 16,* 423-447.

Bateson, G., Jackson, D. D., Haley, J., and Weakland, J. H. (1956). Towards a theory of schizophrenia. *Behavioral Science, 1,* 251-264.

Cartwright, S. (1851). Report on the diseases and physical peculiarities of the Negro race. *New Orleans Medical Surgical Journal, 7,* 692-705.

Center for Health Economics Research (1993). *Access to health care: Key indicators for policy.* Princeton, NJ: Robert Wood Johnson Foundation.

Conrad, D. B. (1871). *First Annual Report of the Central Lunatic Asylum for Colored Insane, 1870-1871.* Richmond, VA: Superintendent of Public Printing.

Dain, N. (1964). *Concepts of insanity in the United States 1789-1865.* New Brunswick, NJ: Rutgers University Press.

Davis, K. (1998). *Slaves don't get stress: The evolution of mental health policies and services for African Americans: Implications for current and future public policy.* Rockville, MD: Center for Mental Health Services.

Davis, K. (2001). The intersection of fee for service, managed health care and cultural competence: Implications for national health care policy and services to people of color. In N. Veeder and W. Peebles-Wilkins (Eds.), *Managed care services: Policies, programs, and research* (pp. 50-73). London: Oxford University Press.

Deutsch, A. (1944). The first U.S. Census of the insane (1840) and its use as pro-slavery propaganda. *Bulletin of the History of Medicine, 15,* 469-482.

Drewry, W. F. (1916). *Central state hospital* (Vol. III) Baltimore: Johns Hopkins Press.

Ennis, B. J. and Siegel, L. (1973). *The rights of mental patients.* New York: Baron Publishers.

Evarts, A. B. (1914). Dementia praecox in the colored race. *Psychoanalytic Review, 1,* 388-403.

Faris, R. and Dunham, H. W. (1939). *Mental disorders in urban areas.* Chicago: University of Chicago Press.

Fischer, J. (1969). Negroes, whites, and rates of mental illness: Reconsideration of a myth. *Psychiatry, 32,* 438-446.

Flaskerud, J. H. and Hu, L. T. (1992). Relationship of ethnicity to psychiatric diagnosis. *Journal of Nervous and Mental Disease, 180,* 296-303.

Focault, M. (1965). *Madness and civilization: A history of insanity in the age of reason.* New York: Vintage.

Garretson, D. J. (1993). Psychological misdiagnosis of African Americans. *Journal of Multicultural Counseling and Development, 21,* 119-126.

Gottesman, I. I. and Shields, J. (1998). *Schizophrenia: The epigenetic puzzle.* New York: Cambridge University Press.

Greenblatt, M., York, R. H., Brown, E. L., and Hyde, R. W. (1955). *From custodial to therapeutic patient care in mental hospitals.* New York: Russell Sage Foundation.

Hollingshead, A. B. and Redlich, F. C. (1958). *Social class and mental illness: A community study.* New York: Wiley.

Hurd, H. M., Drewry, W. F., Dewey, R., Pilgrim, C. W., Blumer, G. A., and Burgess, T. J. W. (1916). *The institutional care of the insane in the United States and Canada.* H. M. Hurd. [III]. Baltimore: The Johns Hopkins Press.

Institute for Health Policy (1993). *Substance abuse: The nation's number one health problem—Key indicators for policy.* Waltham, MA: Robert Wood Johnson Foundation.

Jackson, D. D. (1960). *The etiology of schizophrenia.* New York: Basic Books.

Jackson, J. S., Brown, T., Williams, D. W., Torres, M., Sellers, S., and Brown, K. (1996). Perceptions and experiences of racism and the physical and mental health status of African Americans: A thirteen-year national panel study. *Ethnicity and Disease, 6,* 132-147.

Jackson, J. S., Neighbors, H. W., and Gurin, P. (1986). Findings from a national survey of black mental health: Implications for practice and training. In M. W. Miranda and H. H. L. Kitano (Eds.), *Mental Health Research and Practice* (pp. 91-115). Washington, DC: U.S. Department of Human Services, National Institute of Mental Health.

Jarvis, E. (1844). Insanity among the colored population of the free states. *American Journal of the Medical Sciences, VII,* 71-83.

Jarvis, E. (1852). Insanity among the colored population of the free states. *American Journal of the Medical Sciences, VII,* 73-75.

Joint Commission on Mental Health (1961). *Action for Mental Health.* New York: Science Editions.

Jones, B. E. and Gray, B. A. (1986). Problems in diagnosing schizophrenia and affective disorders among blacks. *Hospital and Community Psychiatry, 37,* 61-65.

Jones, Q. (2002). *The autobiography of Quincy Jones.* New York: Doubleday.

Kendler, K. S. and Diehl, S. R. (1993). The genetics of schizophrenia: A current genetic-epidemiologic perspective. *Schizophrenia Bulletin, 19,* 261-285.

Kessler, R. C., McGonagle, K. A., Zhao, S., Nelson, C. B., Hughes, M., Eshelman, S., Wittchen, H. U., and Kendler, K. S. (1994). Lifetime and 12-month prevalence of DSM-III-R disorders in the United States. *Archives of General Psychiatry, 51,* 8-19.

Kety, S. S. (1987). The significance of genetic factors in the etiology of schizophrenia: Results from the national study of adoptees in Denmark. *Journal of Psychiatric Research, 21,* 423-429.

Kramer, M., Rosen, B. M., and Willis, E. M. (1973). Definitions and distributions of mental disorders in a racist society. In C. V. Willie, B. M. Kramer, and B. S.

Brown (Eds.), *Racism and mental health* (pp. 353-459). Pittsburgh, PA: University of Pittsburgh Press.

Lawson, W. B., Heplar, H., Holladay, J., and Cuffel, B. (1994). Race as a factor in inpatient and outpatient admissions and diagnosis. *Hospital and Community Psychiatry, 45,* 72-74.

Locke, B. Z., Kramer, M., and Pasamanick, B. A. (1960). *Immigration and insanity.* Washington, DC: Public Health Reports.

Malzberg, B. (1953). Mental diseases among Negroes in New York State, 1939-41. *Mental Hygiene, 37,* 450-476.

Malzberg, B. (1959). Mental disease among Negroes: An analysis of first admissions in New York State, 1949-1951. *Mental Hygiene, 43,* 422-459.

Malzberg, B. (1963). Mental disease among Negroes. In M. M. Grossack (Ed.), *Mental Health and Segregation* (pp. 158-160). New York: Springer.

Malzberg, B. and Lee, E. S. (1956). *Migration and mental disease: A study of first admissions to hospitals for mental disease, New York 1939-41.* New York: Social Science Research Council.

Manderscheid, R. W. and Sonnenschein, M. A. (1987). *Mental Health, United States, 1987.* Rockville, MD: U.S. Department of Health and Human Services.

McCandless, P. (1996). *Moonlight, magnolias, and madness: Insanity in South Carolina from the colonial period to the progressive era.* Chapel Hill, NC: University of North Carolina Press.

Morais, H. M. (1967). *The history of the Negro in medicine.* New York: Publishers Co.

Neighbors, H. W. (1984). The distribution of psychiatric morbidity: A review and suggestions for research. *Community Mental Health Journal, 20,* 5-18.

Neighbors, H. W. and Jackson, J. S. (1996). *Mental health in black America.* Thousand Oaks, CA: Sage Publications.

Neighbors, H. W., Jackson, J., Campbell, L., and Williams, D. (1989). The influence of racial factors on psychiatric diagnosis: A review and suggestions for research. *Community Mental Health Journal, 25,* 301-311.

Neighbors, H. W. and Lumpkin, S. (1990). The epidemiology of mental disorder in the black population. In D. S. Ruiz and J. P. Comer (Eds.), *Handbook of mental health and mental disorder among black Americans* (pp. 55-70). New York: Greenwood Press.

O'Malley, M. (1914). Insanity in the colored race. *Journal of Insanity, 71,* 309-336.

Parker, S. and Kleiner, R. J. (1966). *Mental illness in the urban ghetto community.* Glencoe, IL: The Free Press.

Pasamanick, B. A. (1963a). Mental disease among Negroes. In M. M. Grossack (Ed.), *Mental health and segregation* (pp. 150-157). New York: Springer.

Pasamanick, B. A. (1963b). Some misconceptions concerning differences in the racial prevalence of mental disease. *Orthopsychiatry, 33,* 72-86.

Pasamanick, B. A., Lemkau, P. V., Robers, D., and Kruger, D. E. (1960). *A survey of mental disease in an urban population III: Prevalence and demographic dis-*

tribution of some "psychosomatic" disorders (First edition). Washington, DC: American Psychiatric Association.

Ramm, D. (1989). Overcommitted. *Southern Exposure,* Fall, 14-17.

Regier, D. A., Farmer, M. E., Rae, D. S., Meyers, J. K., Kramer, M., Robins, L. N., George, L. K., Karno, M., and Locke, B. Z. (1993). One-month prevalence of mental disorders in the United States and sociodemographic characteristics: The epidemiologic catchment area study. *Acta Psychiatrica Scandinavica, 88,* 35-47.

Riessman, F., Cohn, J., and Pearl, A. (1964). *Mental health of the poor.* New York: Free Press.

Robert Wood Johnson Foundation (1991). *Challenges in health care: A chartbook perspective.* Princeton, NJ: Robert Wood Johnson Foundation.

Robins, L. N. and Regier, D. A. (1991). *Psychiatric disorders in America: The epidemiological catchment area study.* New York: Free Press.

Rose, A. (1955). *Mental health and mental disorder.* New York: Norton Press.

Rothman, D. (1970). *The discovery of the asylum.* Boston: Little, Brown.

Sadler, W. S. (1936). *The theory and practice of psychiatry.* St. Louis: C. V. Mosby Co. Publishers.

Scheffler, R. M. (1991). Differences in mental health service utilization among ethnic subpopulations. *International Journal of Law and Psychiatry, 14,* 363-376.

Segal, S. P., Bola, J. R., and Watson, M. A. (1996). Race, quality of care, and antipsychotic prescribing practices in psychiatric emergency services. *Psychiatric Services, 47,* 282-286.

Snowden, L. (1982). *Reaching the underserved: Mental health needs of neglected populations.* Beverly Hills, CA: Sage Publications.

Snowden, L. and Cheung, F. (1990). Use of inpatient mental health services by members of minority groups. *American Psychologist, 45,* 291-298.

Takeuchi, D. T. and Cheung, M. K. (1998). Coercive and voluntary referrals: How ethnic minority adults get into mental health treatment. *Ethnicity and Health, 3,* 149-158.

Takeuchi, D. T., Sue, S., and Yeh, M. (1995). Return rates and outcomes from ethnic specific and outcomes from ethnic specific mental health programs in Los Angeles. *American Journal of Public Health, 85,* 638-643.

Takeuchi, D. T. and Uehara, E. S. (1996). Ethnic minority mental health services: Current research and future conceptual directions. In B. L. Levin and J. Petrila (Eds.), *Mental health services: A public health perspective* (pp. 63-80). New York: Oxford University Press.

Thomas, A. and Sillen, S. (1972). *Racism and psychiatry.* New York: Brunner/Mazel, Inc.

Torrey, E. F. (1988). *Nowhere to go: The tragic odyssey of the homeless mentally ill.* New York: Harper and Row.

U.S. Department of Health and Human Services (1999). *Mental health: A report of the Surgeon General.* Rockville, MD: U.S. Department of Health and Human Services, SAMHSA, and NIMH.

U.S. Department of Health and Human Services (2001). *Mental health: Culture, race, and ethnicity: A supplement to Mental Health: A Report of the Surgeon General.* Rockville, MD: U.S. Department of Health and Human Services, Substance Abuse and Mental Health Services Administration, Center for Mental Health Services.

Willie, C., Kramer, M., and Brown, B. (1973). *Racism and mental health.* Pittsburgh, PA: University of Pittsburgh Press.

Witmer, A. H. (1891). Insanity in the colored race in the United States. *Alienist and Neurologist, 12,* 19-30.

Chapter 7

African-American Women and Health Disparities: Implications of Race, Class, and Gender

Shelia L. Clark

African-American women's health is in a state of crisis, and where women are in crisis, so are their families and communities. African-American women shoulder the unfair and uneven burdens of death, disability, and disease in this country, having the highest mortality rates of all racial/ethnic groups of women for nearly every major cause of death (National Center for Health Statistics, 1999). African-American women have a life expectancy roughly six years less than that of white women, seventy-four years and eighty years respectively (The Commonwealth Fund, 1999b). Although the overall health of the American people has increased, advances in public health practices and medical technology have not translated into better health outcomes for African-American women. Although the health of mainstream American women should not necessarily be the benchmark or the gold standard for evaluating good health and well-being, the glaring disparities yielded in these kinds of comparisons are beyond compelling, quantifiably demonstrating the significance and severity of health disparities experienced by African-American women, the measure and magnitude of which is appalling. The following narrative, though not exhaustive with respect to the full scope of health indicators, highlights selected health considerations.

Young African-American women have the highest HIV-infection and death rates of any group in the United States (CDC, 2000). Although African-American women comprise only 13.1 percent of the United States population, they have had the most dramatic increases in HIV/AIDS cases, constituting nearly two-thirds (63 percent) of all women reported with AIDS (CDC, 2001). Mortality rates resulting from breast cancer also disproportionately affect African-American women. Although white women are more likely to develop breast cancer, African-American women are most likely to die from the disease (The Commonwealth Fund, 1999b). African-American women are also plagued with disproportionate rates of death from heart disease—death rates are 152.5 deaths per 100,000 for African-American women compared to the national heart disease death rate of 91.1 deaths per 100,000 for white women (National Center for Health Statistics, 1999). African-American women also fare worse on indicators related to cardiovascular disease, including obesity and diabetes. Maternal mortality and infant mortality rates are also shockingly high for African-American women. African-American women are four times more likely than white women to die as a result of pregnancy related complications, and their babies are twice as likely to die (The Commonwealth Fund, 1999b). African-American women also have disparate experiences related to morbidity. A higher proportion of African-American women report experiencing limitations in their activities that directly resulted from a chronic condition (17.6 percent of African-American women compared to 13.1 percent of white women) (Office of Women's Health, 2000).

Though seldom emerging in the larger public health discourse on health disparities, reproductive health, domestic violence, and mental health are significant considerations for women's health, representing yet additional dimensions in which disparities are evident. Reproductive health is an essential part of the overall health and well-being of women. Reproductive health disparities are experienced by African-American women in disproportionate rates of cervical cancer, sexually transmitted infections, fibroids, and unintended pregnancy (National Women's Law Center, 2001a).

The National Black Women's Health Project identified domestic violence as the number one public health issue for African-American women (Joseph, 1997). Domestic violence is a pervasive threat to women's health, as domestic battery is responsible for more injuries to adult women than any other cause, including accidents and muggings combined (Allison, Ramona, and Slupik, 1996). African-American women are three times more likely than white women to be killed as a result of domestic violence (Violence Policy Center, 2001) and less likely to have geographic and culturally competent access to domestic violence services (Bent-Goodley, 2001; Bent-Goodley, in press). Good mental health is central to overall wellness though often treated separately and differently from physical health concerns. Gender considerations in mental health suggest that women are more likely than men to have problems with depression and anxiety (U.S. Public Health Service, 2001). The fact that chronic physical illness and low income, both of which disproportionately affect African-American women, are risk factors for mental illness (U.S. Public Health Service, 2001), clearly makes the case for concern for the mental health needs of African-American women.

In attempting to understand and ultimately eliminate the health disparities that exist for African-American women, it is imperative that the health disparities are not seen as pathologies inherent in or esoteric to African-American women, as cursory assessments may imply. Much of the mainstream dialogue on racial health disparities has been relegated to a discussion and exploration of socioeconomic factors. Although the importance of socioeconomic status is acknowledged as an appropriate consideration, the exclusive promotion of this perspective does not adequately explain or address the root causes, consequences, and cures for the health problems afflicting African-American women and people of color in general. Any legitimate discourse on racial and gender health disparities must go beyond biomedical and economic interpretations to include an honest assessment of the maltreatment of women and people of color in U.S. society and its subsequent impact on health and well-being. The health disparities experienced by African-American women are in many ways derivatives of discriminatory policies and practices targeted toward people of color and women across the broad social spectrum, including the institution of medicine and the health care delivery system.

This chapter will explore the convergence of race, class, and gender as a relevant framework in the consideration of health disparities for African-American women, allowing an opportunity to examine the relationship between social inequities and discriminatory medical practices, and the resulting disparities that exist in health care access, medical treatments, and health outcomes. In addition, the relative role of policy in mitigating, exacerbating, or eliminating health disparities will be discussed from a historical and contemporary perspective, yielding some plausible possibilities for eradicating health disparities and helping African-American women achieve optimal health.

INCOME, EDUCATION, AND ACCESS

Race matters, gender matters, and money matters in American society. This is a culture that has long segregated itself along lines of race, class, and gender, and there is historic oppression and discrimination against women and people of color, making the African-American woman one of the most marginalized and devalued members of our society (Hill-Collins, 1991). Social institutions are deeply rooted in sexism, racism, and discrimination, and inequities in access for people of color to economic, educational, and employment opportunities have resulted in stark demarcations between the "haves" and the "have-nots," with people/women of color being the majority of the latter (Conley, 1999; Rothman, 1993). The "-ism" experience directly and indirectly impacts the physical and mental health of African-American women, as the inequities created by racist institutions are closely correlated with poor health status.

Scientific study has finally lended itself to the evaluation of the social phenomena of racism and discrimination and its impact on the health of people of color. Experiencing racism and discrimination has negative health consequences and is linked to poor physical and mental health. Studies now show that racist experiences are linked with hypertension in African Americans, psychological stress, lower well-being and self reported illness (U.S. Public Health Service, 2001). Although this connection may not be considered new information to communities of color, this research is paramount, serving to elevate the experiences of people of color from anecdotal information to science-based study, a crucial step in understanding health disparities and holding American society accountable for improving the health of people of color.

The indirect consequences of social inequities are manifested in disparities in income, education, and health care access. People of color and women in this country are consistently overrepresented in poverty rates, and while it is a legitimate consideration in the public health paradigm of evaluating health status, it is important to acknowledge the condition of poverty as strongly connected to discriminatory and inequitable social conditions. People living in poverty have the poorest physical health and mental health status (U.S. Public Health Service, 2001). Nearly 24.3 percent of African-American women live in poverty (National Women's Law Center, 2001a). Disparities in wage earnings clearly show inequities as a function of gender and race—women overall earn less than men, 72 cents for every dollar. African-American women only earn 65 cents to every dollar earned by white men (National Women's Law Center, 2001b). People who are poor are more likely to live in more stressful environments, replete with violence, drugs, unemployment, and the like, and are less likely to have social and material resources to buffer negative consequences (U.S. Public Health Service, 2001).

Educational attainment, or lack thereof, is also a contributing factor in health status outcomes for African-American women. High school completion is associated with higher levels of employment and income as well as overall literacy skills which impact one's ability to gain access to, and appropriately navigate, the health care system (The Commonwealth Fund, 1999a). African-American women are less likely to have a high school diploma, 77.4 percent compared to 87 percent of white women (National Women's Law Center, 2001a). This numerical representation of diplomas attained does not speak to the variable quality and availability of educational options in low-income communities which are primarily composed of people of color.

Access to health care is another variable that impacts health outcomes for African-American women. People of color experience greater difficulties in gaining access to care (Davis, Aguilar, and Jackson, 1998; Gaston et al., 1998). Access to preventive care is greatly limited by financial resources and the availability of resources and localized systems of care (National Women's Law Center, 2001a). Nearly two of five (39 percent) African-American adults compared to one of four (26 percent) white adults report not having a regular physician. African Americans are also nearly twice as likely to report having "very little" or "no choice" in where to go for medical care (The Commonwealth Fund, 1999b).

Access to health insurance is often the determining factor in obtaining health care services. Of the roughly 41 million Americans who are uninsured, a substantial number are women (The Henry J. Kaiser Family Foundation, 1998). Approximately one in seven women are uninsured (National Women's Law Center, 2001a). Nearly 33 percent of African-American women lack coverage compared to 21 percent of white women (The Henry J. Kaiser Family Foundation, 1998). Uninsured women are more likely to have hardships in obtaining needed health care services and may forego preventive care (The Commonwealth Fund, 1999a), all considerations for the lagging health status of African-American women.

HEALTH CARE PRACTICES AND POLICIES

The institution of medicine is not immune to racism, discrimination, and sexism, but is rather an active player in perpetuating the politics of race, class, and gender. The history of abuse and exploitation of people of color and women by the medical community, and the general indifference to the health of women and people of color can not be denied (Gaston et al., 1998).

Historical and contemporary examples of racist medical practices and policies exemplify this. The Tuskegee Experiment, perhaps the most notable historical example of racist practices in medicine, displayed the inhumane and purposeful exploitation of African-American men and the lack of regard for their health and for them as persons. African-American women and low-income women have been the subject of abusive and coercive medical policies relating to their reproductive health and their reproductive capacity. Specific practices and policies relate to government-sponsored programs of forced sterilization of African-American and other women of color (Roberts, 1997).

The historical use of involuntary sterilization reflects an ideology that African Americans have too many children, and that this is the etiology of social problems they experience (Roberts, 1997). During the 1970s, federally sponsored mass involuntary sterilization programs and laws were targeted at low-income women and women of color (Roberts, 1997). Between 100,000 and 150,000 poor women, half of whom were African American, were annually sterilized as a part of this program. Other related examples of discriminatory practices include the coercive use of long-acting reproductive technologies such as Norplant and Depo-Provera as methods of population control (Roberts, 1997).

The issue of substance abuse and pregnancy and the treatment of African-American women further reveals discriminatory treatment of African-American women by the medical community and other social systems. Criminally prosecuting women after giving birth to babies who test positive for drugs is a growing trend. Racial bias exists in this practice as health care professionals are much more likely to report African-American women's drug use to government authorities than similar drug use by wealthy white patients (Roberts, 1991). Hospital screening practices result in disproportionate reporting of poor African-American women. Private physicians who serve more affluent women perform less drug screening (Roberts, 1991). Although often debated as a moral issue, substance abuse and pregnancy is a woman's health and public health concern. The punitive nature of current reporting practices is less focused on the provision of health and drug treatment services, and the socioeconomic and psychosocial factors that are associated with maternal substance abuse (Carten, 1996; Nelson-Zlupko, Kauffman, and Dore, 1995).

Other examples from the medical community indicate unequal treatment in the provision of medical treatments for people of color and women. African-American women are the least likely to be referred for cardiac catheterization, less than 40 percent compared to referrals for white men (Schulman et al., 1999). African-American women and men with chronic renal failure are less likely to be referred for transplants and are less likely to receive curative surgery for early-stage lung, colon, and breast cancer (Freeman, 2000). African-American and Latino patients with severe pain are less likely than whites to be able to obtain commonly prescribed pain medicines because pharmacies in predominately nonwhite communities do not carry adequate stocks of opiates (Freeman, 2000).

The routine exclusion of and/or underrepresentation of people of color and women in medical research is also a key factor in considering disparities. Research provides opportunities to consider population differentials in treatment responses and to gain increased knowledge of "best practice" opportunities not maximized for people of color. This creates gaps and deficits in research for African-American women and people of color in general.

Disparate Representation of People of Color in Medicine

Just as there are disparities in the treatment of African Americans and women by the health care system, there are disparities in the number of providers of color within those same systems. People of color are greatly underrepresented in areas of medical education, health care delivery, and research. Although African Americans, Latinos, and Native Americans comprise nearly a quarter (24 percent) of the American population, only 7 percent of physicians, 5 percent of dentists, and 6 percent of medical school faculties are from one of these groups of color; yet the rate of new entrants from these groups is declining (The Commonwealth Fund, 1999b). This is relevant in that physicians of color are more likely to care for underserved populations. Racial similarities between patient and physician also have some bearing on health care satisfaction (The Commonwealth Fund, 1999b).

Clinician Bias in Service Delivery

Another impact of discrimination in health care relates to clinician bias and its impact on how African Americans perceive and receive care. A survey conducted by the Commonwealth Fund found that 43 percent of African Americans and 28 percent of Latinos, compared to 5 percent of whites, felt that a doctor or health care provider had judged or treated them unfairly or with disrespect because of their race or ethnic background (U.S. Public Health Service, 2001). Medical service providers are individuals in a collective community responsible for the provision of care. Practitioners, who may be impacted by personal and societywide misconceptions, attitudes, and discriminatory views of African Americans, can practice in a manner that translates into mis-, under-, or overdiagnosis of certain health problems, and inappropriately administer treatment practices and referrals (U.S. Public Health Service, 2001). African Americans are often overdiagnosed for the most severe mental health conditions and underdiagnosed for pervasive problems such as depression. People of color are less likely to receive the best treatments for depression (U.S. Public Health Service, 2001). This is again especially important for African-American women, as women in general are more likely to suffer from depression.

The treatment of people of color and women by service providers can impact the level of mistrust on the part of people of color and impact treatment seeking behaviors. African Americans are less likely to pursue medical treatment, seek preventive care, participate in medical research, and to participate in organ donation (Randall, 1996).

HEALTH POLICY AND AFRICAN-AMERICAN WOMEN: OPPORTUNITIES TO ADVANCE BLACK WOMEN'S HEALTH

Policy is a crucial aspect of defining strategies to eliminate health disparities as it can serve to set health priorities, guide medical practice, specify the allocation of resources, and directly address social inequities related to poor health outcomes. Some progressive policy initiatives have emerged that represent significant achievements and strides in reducing racial health disparities for people of color and women.

The topic of racial health disparities has rightfully emerged as part of the dialogue on national health priorities. One of the major national programs that was introduced under the Clinton Administration is the Initiative to Eliminate Racial and Ethnic Disparities (1998), a part of Healthy People 2010, the federal blueprint for improving the nation's health. This initiative articulates a national commitment to eliminate racial health disparities. It focuses on six key areas: (1) infant mortality; (2) cancer screening and management; (3) cardiovascular disease; (4) diabetes; (5) immunizations; and (6) HIV/ AIDS. These represent key areas of disparities for African-American women.

In November 2000, the Health Care Fairness Act (Public Law 106-525) was passed which amends the Public Health Service Act to expand research and data collection on health disparities that affect people of color and underserved populations. It created the National Center on Minority Health and Health Disparities that will, among other things, direct a comprehensive study of the U.S. Department of Health and Human Services data collection systems and practices on race and ethnicity, and create a research demonstration grant program for training and educating health professionals on disparities and culturally competent health care. This measure was sponsored by Congressional Black Caucus member, Representative Jesse Jackson Jr. (D-IL).

Gender-specific research is paramount to addressing the unique health care needs of women and in 1993, the National Institute of

Health (NIH) Revitalization Act (Public Law 103-43) was passed, legislatively mandating that women and people of color be included in NIH-funded research. Another example of progressive policy is the Breast and Cervical Cancer Treatment Act of 2000, which provides states with the option of providing Medicaid coverage to women who are diagnosed with breast or cervical cancer. The Violence Against Women Act of 2000 (Public Law 106-386) addresses the issue of domestic violence by improving legal tools and programs on domestic violence, sexual assault, and stalking. The Act reauthorizes critical grant programs created by the Violence Against Women Act of 1994 (Public Law 103-322) and subsequent legislation. It also establishes new programs focused on people of color and strengthens federal laws.

Although some progressive policies exist relating to health disparities, they do not go far enough in specifically addressing the health concerns of African-American women and other women of color. Policy and advocacy efforts are failing African-American women and, to date, there exists neither a separate nor integrated health policy agenda for women of color. African-American women's health issues have been diluted in the larger context of the health of women or people of color. This lack of specific national attention through policy and program initiatives represents "disparities within disparities" and it has undermined the ability of African-American women to have complete health and wellness. Just as women are different from men, women of color are different from other women, and this needs to be acknowledged and addressed in the medical research community.

Ultimately, the far-reaching agenda for health promotion must embrace the role of race and gender discrimination in health disparities, and focus on eradicating those barriers to good health that discrimination creates. Racism and discrimination, poverty, and gender bias cannot be accepted social realities, and policymakers and advocates alike must work to eradicate these global social issues. Health and related social polices cannot continue to marginalize people of color while preserving privileged peoples' access to health care and services. There are immeasurable ways in which policy and practice can be altered to achieve better health for African-American women.

1. The convergence of race, class, and gender must be standard considerations in the formulation and implementation of health

and health-related policies and practices. The nature of health disparities and its relation to race, class, and gender make necessary policy actions and practices that eliminate discrimination and consider the social context of poor health outcomes and African-American women's lives.

2. There must be increased representation of people of color in the area of medicine and health research. As clinician bias and discriminatory treatment of people of color relates to and impacts health disparities, increasing the presence of people of color in medicine will serve to create more culturally responsive health care systems. Greater emphasis must be placed on gender and race-based analysis in research and medical interventions. It is important that African-American women are included in larger numbers as principal investigators, leading health research.

3. Health care must be a social justice issue. Health outcomes are intrinsically linked to the social environment, and social inequities result in health disparities. Improvements in health must reflect overall improvements in achieving equity for African-American women and people of color. Equal opportunities for African-American women and for all people of color must be opened up in employment, education, equitable pay, and the like. Racism and discrimination must be targeted wherever it exists, including health care and health policy. Good health and access to medical care must become an issue of civil and human rights.

CONCLUSION

Civil rights, human rights, discrimination, and racism have been issues around which advocates and activists have organized, mobilized, and fought. Racial and gender health disparities must be addressed in the same fashion. Advocates, through their organizational initiatives and discussions, must help reframe the issue of racial health disparities to policymakers and to the public in general. A commitment to eliminating racial and gender health disparities must encompass the health and social concerns of African-American women and people and women of color.

African-American women, and all women and men, have a right to health and wellness, a life free from intimidation and violence, racism, sexism, and discrimination. The complexity of circumstances that surround health disparities must be addressed on a personal and a political level. These issues must receive appropriate national attention and there must be a policy approach that promotes equity for people of color and women across all social institutions. The health of *all* citizens can be valued and promoted, as we strive for a just society where individual differences will be treated equally.

REFERENCES

Allison, K., Ramona, I., and Slupik, R. (1996). *American Medical Association: Complete guide to women's health.* New York: Random House.

Bent-Goodley, T.B. (2001). Eradicating domestic violence in the African American community: A literature review and action agenda. *Trauma, Violence, and Abuse, 2,* 316-330.

Bent-Goodley, T.B. (in press). Perceptions of domestic violence: A dialogue with African-American women. *Health and Social Work.*

Carten, A.J. (1996). Mothers in recovery: Rebuilding families in the aftermath of addiction. *Social Work, 41,* 214-223.

Centers for Disease Control and Prevention (2000). *National data on HIV prevalence among disadvantaged youth in the 1990s.* Atlanta, GA: National Center for HIV, STD, and TB Prevention.

Centers for Disease Control and Prevention (2001). *HIV/AIDS among U.S. women: Minority and young women at continuing risk.* Atlanta, GA: National Center for HIV, STD, and TB Prevention.

The Commonwealth Fund (1999a). *Health insurance coverage and access to care for working-age women.* New York: The Commonwealth Fund.

The Commonwealth Fund (1999b). *U.S. Minority Health: A Chartbook.* New York: The Commonwealth Fund.

Conley, D. (1999). *Being black, living in the red: Race, wealth, and social policy in America.* Berkeley, CA: University of California Press.

Davis, K.E., Aguilar, M.A., and Jackson, V.H. (1998). Save low-income women and their children first. *Health and Social Work, 23,* 83-85.

Freeman, H. (2000). Racial injustice in health care. *The New England Journal of Medicine, 342,* 1045-1047.

Gaston, M.H., Barrett, S.E., Johnson, T.L., and Epstein, L.G. (1998). Health care needs of medically underserved women of color: The Role of the Bureau of Primary Health Care. *Health and Social Work, 23,* 86-95.

The Henry J. Kaiser Family Foundation (1998). *The Kaiser Commission on Medicaid and the uninsured: The uninsured and their access to health care.* Menlo Park, CA: The Henry J. Kaiser Foundation.

The Henry J. Kaiser Family Foundation (1999). *A synthesis of the literature: Racial and ethnic differences in access to medical care.* Menlo Park, CA: The Henry J. Kaiser Family Foundation.

Hill-Collins, P. (1991). *Black feminist thought: Knowledge, consciousness, and the politics of empowerment.* New York: Routledge.

Joseph, J. (1997). Woman battering: A comparative analysis of black and white women. In G.K. Kantor and J.L. Jasinski (Eds.), *Out of darkness: Contemporary perspectives on famiily violence* (pp. 161-169). Thousand Oaks, CA: Sage.

National Center for Health Statistics, Centers for Disease Control and Prevention (1999). *Women's health data by state and U.S. territory: Mortality 1994-1997.* Hyattsville, MD: National Center for Health Statistics, Centers for Disease Control and Prevention.

National Women's Law Center (2001a). Making the grade on women's health: A national and state-by-state report card. Washington, DC: National Women's Law Center. [Online]. Available: <www. http://www.nwlc.org/display.cfm?section=health#(Women's Health Report Card 2001)>.

National Women's Law Center (2001b). The paycheck fairness act: Helping to close the women's wage gap [Online]. Available: <http://www.nwlc.org/display.cfm?section=employment#(Equal Pay)>.

Nelson-Zlupko, L., Kauffman, E., and Dore, M.M. (1995). Gender differences in drug addiction and treatment: Implications for social work intervention with substance-abusing women. *Social Work, 40,* 45-54.

Office of Women's Health (2000). *Minority women's health status* [Online]. Available: <http://www.4women.org/owh/pub/minority/index.htm>.

Randall, V. (1996). Slavery, segregation, and racism: Trusting the health care system ain't always easy—an African American perspective on bioethics. *St. Louis U. Pub. L. Rev, 15,* 191-235 [Online]. Available: <www.udayton.edu/~health/05bioethics/slavery.htm>.

Roberts, D. (1991). Punishing drug addicts who have babies: Women of color, equality, and the right of privacy. *Harvard Law Review, 104,* 1419-1482.

Roberts, D. (1997). *Killing the black body.* New York: Pantheon Books.

Rothman, R.A. (1993). *Inequality and stratification: Class, color, and gender* (Second edition). Englewood Cliffs, NJ: Prentice-Hall.

Schulman, D., Berlin, J., William, H., Kerner, J., Sistrunk, S., Gersh, B., Dube, R., Taleghani, J., Sankey, W., Eisenburg, J., Escarce, J., and Ayers, W. (1999). The effects of race and sex on physicians' recommendations for cardiac catheterization. *New England Journal of Medicine, 340,* 618-628.

U.S. Public Health Service (2001). *Mental health: Culture, race, and ethnicity—A supplement to mental health: A report of the surgeon general.* Rockville, MD:

U.S. Department of Health and Human Services, Substance Abuse and Mental Health Services Administration, Center for Mental Health Services.

Violence Policy Center (2001). *When men kill women: An analysis of 1999 homicide data.* [Online]. Available: <www.vpc.org/studies/dv4cont.htm>.

Chapter 8

Policy Implications of the Criminal Justice System for African-American Families and Communities

Tricia B. Bent-Goodley

More than five million Americans are under some form of correctional supervision, including probation, parole, and incarceration. For some, the criminal justice system has become an individual retirement plan; for others a source of community development and economic vitality. "Total U.S. prison operating costs (federal and state) grew from about $3.1 billion in fiscal year 1980 to more than $17 billion in fiscal year 1994" (Austin and Coventry, 2001, p. 1). Today, about $35 billion is spent annually on corrections (Schlosser, 1998). The number of private prisons has grown to 158 in 1998 and continues to steadily climb (Austin and Coventry, 2001). State prisons are operating at 15 percent over capacity and federal prisons at over 31 percent capacity (Beck and Harrison, 2001). Inmate labor provides "stable, steady income" that is "recession proof" (Schlosser, 1998, p. 58) as inmates are often forced to work for wages between 25 to 40 cents per hour (Isaac, Lockhart, and Williams, 2001). Criminal justice is a booming business in American culture, no longer solely powered by politics and propaganda but also by economics.

African Americans comprised 21 percent of the prison population in 1926 (Mauer, 1999). They currently comprise 46 percent of the prison population, while whites account for 36 percent and Latinos for 16 percent (Beck and Harrison, 2001). The purposes of this chapter are twofold: (1) to illuminate how criminal justice policies negatively impact African Americans, and (2) to structure a plan of action for how social workers can affect the criminal justice system.

CURRENT CRIMINAL JUSTICE STATISTICS

With the second highest incarceration rate in the world (Mauer, 1999), America incarcerates one in every 149 U.S. residents annually (Beck and Mumola, 1999); of these, 94 percent are men. Most (65 percent) have not completed high school, with a 70 percent illiteracy rate (Schlosser, 1998). One-third were unemployed before being arrested and had annual incomes under $5,000. Over half (57 percent) were under the influence of a controlled substance at the time of the offense (Center for Mental Health Services, 1995). Seventy-one percent are imprisoned for a nonviolent crime, including drug offenses (30 percent) and property offenses (31 percent) (Beck and Harrison, 2001; Congressional Quarterly, 2000). One-quarter of jail inmates, 22 percent of state prison inmates, and 59 percent of federal prison inmates are imprisoned for a drug offense. More than 16 percent (over 200,000) inmates have a mental illness (Center for Mental Health Services, 1995; Schlosser, 1998). In fact, "the number of mentally ill behind bars today is nearly five times the number in state mental hospitals" (Branigan and Smith, 2001, p. A1). Immigration offenses have recently increased by 488 percent (Beck and Harrison, 2001). This finding is of great importance to people of color, particularly African Americans and Latinos.

The rising level of incarceration has taken place while serious crime has fallen over the past seven years (Chaiken, 2000; Fields and Johnson, 2000; Schlosser, 1998). The decline in crime rates has been attributed to the strong economy, the eradication of street drug markets, an increased police presence, more after-school programs, and an aging criminal population (Fields and Johnson, 2000). The recurrent myth that incarceration discourages crime is false, as evidenced by crime rates being worse in places with higher incarceration rates.

Women and the Criminal Justice System

More than 91,612 women are in U.S. state and federal prisons and jails (Beck and Harrison, 2001). Since 1990, the annual growth rate for imprisoning women has been higher on average than men (Beck and Mumola, 1999; Conly, 1998). A 77 percent growth rate of male prisoners has occurred since 1990, whereas, for the same period the growth rate for women prisoners has been 108 percent (Beck and Harrison, 2001). Well over 75 percent of these women have been convicted for a nonviolent offense (Kurshan, 1999) or simple assaults (Greenfield and Snell, 1999). Seventy-five percent of these women are mothers (Beckerman, 1994; Conly, 1998; Kurshan, 1999), with an estimate of over a quarter of a million children growing up having a mother who is incarcerated (Young and LoMonaco, 2001). This is particularly significant as these women were often the primary caretakers of their children prior to incarceration (Beckerman, 1994; Conly, 1998). Their children are two to six times more likely to end up in prison than the children of male prisoners.

Harlow (1999) found that 51 to 77 percent of women in state prisons, jail, or on probation had been abused by an intimate partner. Twenty-five percent of these women were sexually abused as children, with 86.7 percent of them growing up in foster care and with 75 percent having parents who were substance abusers (Harlow, 1999). Approximately 33 percent of these women become homeless once released from prison or jail.

Drug violation arrests have nearly tripled for women (Bush-Baskette, 1998). Incarcerated women tend to have few job skills, little or no work experience, substance abuse problems, are young, unmarried, victims of abuse, and have high rates of HIV infection (Danner, 1998; Henriques and Manatu-Rupert, 2001; Van Wormer and Bartollas, 2000). Women that are chemically dependent have fewer social networks, experience greater problems in receiving treatment due to child care issues, and often begin using a substance due to a traumatic event (Nelson-Zlupko, Kauffman, and Dore, 1995). "Substance abuse among women in prison is often tangled up with histories of mental illness (co-occurring disorders); sexual and physical abuse; poverty; and living as unemployed, single mothers with few coping skills and little social or family support" (Chandler and Kassebaum, 1997, p. 163). In 1997, at least 2,300 women (6 percent) were pregnant upon entering prison and their crimes were often committed to obtain money for drugs (Conly, 1998). Within twenty-four to seventy-two hours after the birth of their children, these women are separated from their babies who often end up in foster or kinship care (Kurshan, 1999).

African Americans and the Criminal Justice System

The majority of African-American families have never come in contact with the criminal justice system (Hill, 1997). The vast majority do not have daughters who are using drugs or committing property offenses. Their sons are not drug dealers and wife beaters and their young children are not out robbing others and committing burglaries. The majority of African-American men and women are obtaining a college education and making positive contributions to their communities and larger society. Yet, if one person suffers or creates suffering, the entire community is affected. Consequently, understanding the plight of those impacting and affected by the criminal justice system is critical for everyone, as all individuals are connected.

It has been stated that African Americans commit more crimes than the general public, constituting differential involvement in criminal activity (Blumstein, 1982; Langan, 1985). Blumstein later acknowledges that racial disproportions cannot be solely explained by African Americans committing more crimes than the general population (Blumstein, 1993). Blumstein, as cited in Russell, "readily acknowledges that 20 to 25 percent of the incarceration rate for Blacks is not explained by disproportionate offending" (Russell, 1998, p. 31). Mauer (1999) asserts that this percentage, equivalent to about 10,000 African Americans that are incarcerated, is woefully low. African Americans are no more likely to commit crimes than other racial or ethnic groups but are more likely to be prosecuted and receive longer sentences due, in large part, to racism and classism (Russell, 1998; Mauer, 1999; Wilson, 1990; The Sentencing Project, 2000). Gibbs and Bankhead (2001) discuss more intensive "police surveillance" (p. 60) in urban communities as one reason for differential arrest rates. It is clear that more empirical research, conducted in a culturally competent fashion, needs to be conducted in this area.

African Americans are seven times more likely to be incarcerated than whites (Mauer, 1999). Although white men stand a 4 percent chance of being imprisoned over the course of their lives, African-American men have a 28 percent chance of imprisonment. These statistics can be explained not by differential involvement but by racism and discrimination. The sociohistorical context is crucial to understanding why African Americans experience the criminal justice system in such large numbers (Alridge and Daniels, 2001). African-

American men are convicted of drug felonies 52 percent of the time, while white men are convicted for drug felonies only 34 percent of the time (Weich and Angulo, 2000).

> In 1976, Blacks constituted 22 percent of the arrest rates in the United States for drug abuse violations (as compared to 77 percent for Whites). By 1990, the percentage of arrests involving Blacks nationwide had risen to 41 percent and had decreased to 59 percent for Whites. (Bush-Baskette, 1998, p. 114)

Young African-American and Latino men receive harsher sentences than middle-aged white men who commit the same crimes (Spohn and Holleran, 2000). Those who are unemployed and of color receive harsher sentences than those who are employed and white (Spohn and Holleran, 2000). The economics of the criminal justice system is frightening. Sampson (1987) found that crime rates and violence increased in poor communities largely when unemployment rates rose and job prospects remained bleak. Crutchfield, Glusker, and Bridges (1999) found that the labor market, education, and poverty converged to explain chronic disadvantage leading to higher homicide rates in poorer communities. They advocate looking beyond employment to labor market changes, such as labor instability and "the stratification of labor into primary and secondary sector jobs" (p. 65). Their findings are reinforced by Krivo and Peterson (1996), who reinforce that the influence of structural disadvantage is significant when considering crime in urban communities. Structural disadvantage includes high poverty levels, social isolation, and economically segregated communities.

Recent trends have witnessed an increase in the incarceration rate of African-American women. African-American women are six times more likely than white women and three times more likely than Latinas to go to prison, although white women are arrested in greater numbers. Today, "Black women constitute a greater proportion of the incarcerated female population than do Black males of the incarcerated male population" (Bush-Baskette, 1998, p. 119). African-American women are also more likely to serve longer sentences (Isaac, Lockhart, and Williams, 2001). The rising rate of incarceration of African-American women is largely explained by the war on drugs and mandatory minimum sentencing (Bush-Baskette, 1998). "Between

1986 and 1991, the incarceration rate for drug offenses for African-American women increased nearly twice as fast as for African-American males—828 percent over 429 percent" (Locy, 1999, p. 18) with 60 percent serving time for a drug offense. Domestic and sexual violence has also been a key reason for the incarceration of women, and African-American women in particular (Van Wormer and Bartollas, 2000). In a study conducted by Richie (2000), "40 percent of women in a large urban jail had experienced violence at the hands of an intimate partner, and 35 percent reported sexual abuse" (pp. 5-6). The complexity of issues, such as sexual abuse, domestic violence, sexism, and classism, must be fully examined and understood to effectively address this trend.

Juvenile Justice

In 1988 the federal government mandated that states "address the problem of minority overrepresentation in the juvenile justice system" (Lundman, 2001, p. 129). African-American youths are incarcerated at five times the rate of white youths (Juszkiewicz, 2000). They are overrepresented in detention caseloads, disproportionately confined, more likely to be held in public custody, and have a longer length of stay once incarcerated than white youths (Bilchik, 1999). Of those youths who are charged in adult courts, 82 percent are of color (Juszkiewicz, 2000) and they are more likely than white children to be waived to adult courts (Cose, 2000).

Hearing these statistics one would suspect that African-American children and other children of color commit more crimes than white children. Yet "arrests of White juveniles (under age 18) constituted 71 percent of all juvenile arrests—compared with 26 percent for Black youth" (Hawkins et al., 2000, p. 2). White youths are two times as likely to have charges reduced to misdemeanor status (Juszkiewicz, 2000). Although there is a decline in the number of African-American youths using drugs, 38 percent are arrested for drug offenses and 59 percent are convicted (Weich and Angulo, 2000). "African American (43 percent) and Latino youth (37 percent) [are] more likely than White youth (26 percent) to receive a sentence of incarceration (as opposed to a split sentence or probation)" (Juszkiewicz, 2000, p. 10).

African Americans, particularly youths, are less likely to be represented by private counsel (Juszkiewicz, 2000). They are more likely to live in poverty, have a single mother, and no job prospects (Hawkins et al., 2000; Lundman, 2001). A greater number of these young people are exiting foster or group care without sufficient resources and support, resulting in increasing juvenile incarceration rates (Jonson-Reid and Barth, 2000; Locy, 1999). An alarming increase in female juvenile justice offenders exists, with young girls accounting for 25 percent of juvenile arrests and cases (Poe-Yamagata and Butts, 1996); yet there are limited gender-specific services for these girls, demonstrating a system full of gender bias (McDonald and Chesney-Lind, 2001). The juvenile justice system is an area warranting greater research and advocacy.

MAJOR CRIMINAL JUSTICE ISSUES FOR AFRICAN AMERICANS

The War on Drugs and Mandatory Minimum Sentencing

The war on drugs has been in effect a war on people of color, particularly African Americans (Bush-Baskette, 1998; Taifa, in press). Coupled with multiple criminal justice policies, the impact of the war on drugs has profoundly affected the African-American family and community. The Rockefeller Drug Laws, enacted in New York State in 1973, provided the basis for most changes in drug laws across the country, as it imposed a fifteen-year to life mandatory minimum sentence for possessing four ounces or selling two ounces of a narcotic substance. As a bellwether state, many other states used this policy to inform their plan of action against crime. The result has been a substantial increase in incarceration rates, particularly for women. Ninety-five percent of women sentenced after the Rockefeller Drug Laws had no prior criminal history and were often forced or tricked into committing a crime.

The Controlled Substances Act (21 U.S.C. 841) and the Controlled Substances Import and Export Act (21 U.S.C. 960) largely established the crack/cocaine disparity in sentencing. The policy established a ten-year mandatory minimum sentence (MMS) for anyone convicted of selling five kilograms of powder cocaine or 50 milligrams of crack cocaine and a five-year mandatory minimum sentence for anyone convicted of selling 500 grams of powder cocaine or five grams of crack cocaine. This policy has had a disproportionately negative impact on poor communities and communities of color because 92.6 percent of crack cocaine users are African American and 45.2 percent of powder cocaine users are white (Blumstein, 2001).

The Anti-Drug Abuse Act of 1986 (PL 99-570) revived federal MMS, which had been voted down in 1970. Mandatory minimum sentencing takes power away from " judges to exercise discretion on behalf of defendants in order to check prosecutorial discretion" (Weich and Angulo, 2000, p. 21). In essence, once the prosecutor decides the charge, if convicted the defendant will serve a predetermined sentence. Mandatory minimum sentencing has been particularly harmful to women and people of color, resulting in the rise in federal and state prison rates (Blumstein, 2001; Chandler and Kassebaum, 1997; Feinman, 1980; Van Wormer and Bartollas, 2000). Because there has been a clear pattern of unfair prosecutorial discretion that negatively impacts African Americans and Latinos, MMS is extremely troublesome (Weich and Angulo, 2000).

It is important to note that a critique of these policies does not denote support for drug selling. The influx of drugs, particularly in communities of color, has clearly been detrimental to strong communities and healthy, intact families. This analysis seeks to illuminate policy inequities that result in harsher and disparate treatment of African Americans in the criminal justice system.

Three Strikes Law

The Three Strikes Law states that "defendants with two prior criminal convictions can be sentenced to life in prison, even if their third strike is for relatively minor conduct" (Weich and Angulo, 2000, p. 22). First initiated in 1994 as Proposition 194 in California (Gibbs and Bankhead, 2001), this policy was intended to focus on repeat violent offenders by imposing a twenty-five year to life sentence for the third conviction, including juvenile offenses. The impact of this policy has been the incarceration of greater numbers of nonviolent individuals and an increase in the long-term care of prisoners (Dickey and Hollenhorst, 1999). By 1999 in California, "one-half of the more than 5,000 defendants who had received life sentences were nonviolent offenders" (Gibbs and Bankhead, 2001, p. 64), who were not the intended focus of the policy. The constitutionality of the three strikes law is currently being debated in the Supreme Court in the case of *Ewing v. California* (No. 01-6978) (Lane, 2002).

Again the intent of this chapter is not to indicate that committing crimes should be allowed nor that individuals should be enabled to continuously commit crimes without consequences. However, when it is clear that a policy is not meeting its purpose and that it is resulting in the differential and unfair treatment of any citizen, then it becomes the responsibility of every citizen to advocate for change.

Racial Profiling and Police Brutality

Two separate issues, racial profiling and policy brutality, speak to the ways in which policy interacts with citizens. Racial profiling has been defined as "the identification of potential criminal suspects on the basis of skin color or accent" (Cole, 1999, p. 1). One study in Maryland found that while African Americans constitute 17.5 percent of motorists, they compose 70 percent of those stopped on the highway, resulting in less than 8 percent of arrests (Weich and Angulo, 2000). Racial profiling is also called "driving while black" (DWB) and results in a growing group of African Americans that are cynical and fearful of the police (Johnson, 2001; Langan et al., 2001). Langan et al. (2001) also found that African Americans were more likely to be stopped by police; however, in order to prove that racial profiling exists one would need to demonstrate that "Blacks were no more likely than Whites to violate traffic laws" and that "police pulled over Blacks at a higher rate than Whites" (p. 13). Impacting one's sense of safety and security, racial profiling goes beyond being angry about being targeted. It evokes frustration and anxiety in the open acknowledgment that there is continued overt racism in America that goes without punishment or recognition as a crime in and of itself.

Police brutality has similar effects within communities of color. Fear of police, anger, and mistrust result in the decision not to reach out to law enforcement at times when it is appropriate and can make individuals anxious when they see a police presence even when they have done nothing wrong (Chaiken, 2000). One young person stated he felt as if he were "prey to the police" (Cose, 2000, p. 43). With so many acts of police brutality that go unpunished (Duke, 2000), some communities feel as if there is nowhere to turn for justice. These types of police officers make the entire system appear corrupt. Police officers are more likely to report serious conduct and that willingness to report negative behavior is largely based on the organizational culture (Klockars et al., 2000). Yet the definition of "serious conduct" is unique to individual precincts or stations. Police officers, supervisors, and other officials who condone this brutality through their silence or assistance must be replaced with caring, capable officers, supervisors, and management concerned for safety, high ethical conduct, and strong community relations.

It is important to mention that while these fears and mistrust are valid based on the historical and current realities, one cannot stereotype all of law enforcement. The fact that individuals put their lives at risk each day to save lives is a tremendous sacrifice for the individuals and their families. The overwhelming number of police that go to work and provide counseling, guidance, and protection to others should not be discounted. This can be demonstrated by the heroic acts of police officers who gave their lives on September 11, 2001. Yet, we must advocate for the dismissal and reprimand of those that continue to break the public trust through disrespect and discriminatory treatment on the street and behind closed doors where decisions are made.

Death Penalty

The intention of this section is not to argue for or against the death penalty but instead to point out the systemic issues that should be of grave concern to all Americans regardless of their position on this issue. The inequity and false incarceration of African Americans and others is well documented (Congressional Quarterly, 2000; Johnson, 2001; Liebman, Fagan, and West, 2000; Weich and Angulo, 2000).

African Americans are four times more likely to receive the death penalty than whites. African Americans make up a disproportionate number of inmates on death row with 42 percent of those on death row being African American (Liebman, Fagan, and West, 2000). Interestingly, 38 percent of death row inmates have been freed since 1973 due to their convictions being overturned. In 2000, "58 persons' sentences were overturned or removed" (Snell, 2001, p. 9). Between 1977 and 2000, 41 percent of those persons receiving a sentence of death were African American (Snell, 2001). Sadly, 35 percent of those inmates executed and later found to be innocent of the charges were African American. These statistics point to a system that is executing, far too many times, innocent people without regard for their lives or their innocence.

"Over 100 innocent Americans have been exonerated from death row in just the last two decades, but not before losing a total of over 800 years of their lives on death row for crimes they didn't commit" (The Moratorium Campaign, 2002b). Although almost 80 percent of executions took place in the South in 2001, the South continues to have the highest murder rate in the country (The Moratorium Campaign, 2002a). Thus, capital punishment does not deter crime. Currently, Maryland and Illinois have a moratorium on the death penalty, in an effort to study the implementation of the death penalty in the respective states. Maryland's incoming Republican governor Robert L. Ehrlich Jr. has already stated that he will rescind the execution moratorium, without consideration of an impending report on the implementation of the death penalty in Maryland (Montgomery, 2002). Eleven states do not use the death penalty at all. The Supreme Court is also examining issues around capital punishment in the case of *Wiggins v. Corcoran,* where the inadequacy of legal counsel is being examined as it relates to poor representation and sentencing outcomes (The Moratorium Campaign, 2002b). The death penalty goes beyond moral arguments to the continued pervasiveness of racism and discrimination of people of color and poor people in America.

Impact of Criminal Justice Policies on Families

The impact of these policies has been detrimental and catastrophic. Nearly 1.5 million children have an incarcerated parent, with African-American children being nine times more likely than white children to have a parent in prison (Mumola, 2000). More than 50 percent of women in prison never see their children; approximately 25 percent of these children go into nonrelative foster care. The absence of a parent, due to incarceration, negatively impacts children (Beckerman, 1994; Danner, 1998; Young and LoMonaco, 2001). Social workers have been found not to connect mothers in prison with their children, compounding the problem (Beckerman, 1994).

Over fifty percent of these children are placed with a grandparent (generally a grandmother) who is already overburdened and financially stressed (Locy, 1999; Mumola, 2000). Many kin providers have limited fiscal and social resources and are often denied similar benefits as nonrelative foster care providers, particularly if they are not willing to legally adopt the child. Too many kin providers are forced to exhaust all of their assets before being eligible to receive or becoming aware of public funds. Some end up having to obtain TANF in order to simply survive. The limited support, financial and otherwise, for these kin providers is criminal in and of itself.

Children are often left to grieve the loss of the parent with limited support and understanding. The children may be experiencing post-traumatic stress disorder, depression, guilt, anger, fear, relief, abandonment, and confusion. Yet, there are limited services offered to these often fragile families. The children are rarely asked about what they are experiencing because social workers either feel ill-prepared to address the response or do not recognize the problem (Beckerman, 1994; Snyder-Joy and Carlo, 1998). Based on a number of the common characteristics of offenders identified earlier in this chapter, the children have often witnessed the effects of substance abuse, violence, poverty, and potentially have been abused themselves.

These are merely some of the ways incarceration impacts the immediate family. Other issues to consider include the loss of income, anxiety of what could happen to the person incarcerated, the struggle of dealing with the absence of the person, and the anger over the crime committed (Cose, 2000). While these inmates may have committed a crime, there is often a family left to deal with the pain of both the loss and the crime. The children are often the most innocent and least likely to receive assistance. If rightfully convicted, it is acknowledged that the inmate made a choice to commit the crime; however, those family members innocent of the offense should not also systemically be forced to pay the price.

Impact on the Community

The community impact of the criminal justice system is also significant. Ex-offenders and parolees often return to the community more disconnected than when they left. "In high crime communities that are socially isolated and racially segregated, . . . locking up even more people may be so damaging to neighborhood social cohesion that it destabilizes the very areas it is supposed to make safe" (Cose, 2000, p. 44). Increasingly, the impact of inmates returning to communities with high rates of HIV infection and infected individuals knowingly or unknowingly poses serious threats to the public health of the community (Fullilove, 2000).

Often unable to secure employment or obtain TANF, these individuals are relegated either back into poverty or the lifestyle that led to incarceration. Ineligible for financial aid, they are limited in the ability to advance the education that could assist them in making contributions to society (Tewksbury, Erickson, and Taylor, 2000). Thus, there is less economic development within these communities and far less social and human capital invested.

When fully fed up and desiring to change these policies, the ex-felony offender will often find that he or she is unable to vote (CBCF News, 2001; Chaiken, 2000). Currently, there are thirty-two states that deny felony offenders on probation, parole, or released from prison the right to vote and ten states have actually disenfranchised ex-offenders for life (Human Rights Watch and The Sentencing Project, 1998). Consequently, 1.4 million African-American men lack the right to vote; that is, 13 percent of African-American men have been disenfranchised (Weich and Angulo, 2000). The right to vote provides people of color with one of few routes to power.

Interestingly, prison populations add to the census numbers in the areas they occupy. Consequently, many prisoners add to the resources and political clout of the very politicians supporting their incarceration and the incarceration of those that look like them. There are many rural communities that benefit from the incarceration of individuals from urban environments. This paradox takes away from those urban communities where the very resources that could assist them in limiting the number of incarcerated individuals is actually being shifted to rural communities that are growing based on the continued supply from the inner city. Without voting power, communities are often ignored and not perceived as a priority. With so many African-American men disenfranchised, their communities are also left powerless.

IMPLICATIONS

Recommitment from the Social Work Profession

Criminal justice was once a priority for the profession; however, since 1965 it has been largely de-emphasized as a significant area of social work practice (Corcoran and Shireman, 1997). Although a vast number of social workers continue to work in the area (Hickman, 2000; Roberts, 1997), there is a greater need for the profession to recommit to social justice in the criminal justice arena through advocacy and education. Young and LoMonaco (2001) provide concrete examples of how to integrate criminal justice content throughout the social work curriculum. Current trends reinforce the need for social workers to come back to the table with a more focused, collective agenda. There can be no social justice without dealing effectively with the criminal justice system.

Organizational Cooperation

Clearly the criminal justice system affects child welfare, gerontology, health, mental health, and community development. Practitioners in these areas must learn about how the criminal justice system affects them and their clients.

Greater interagency collaboration is crucial. Court systems should include supportive services within the courts for family members of those incarcerated, with family and child welfare agencies providing important linkages. Thus, family members could access these services and obtain needed referrals in the community for services such as mental health counseling and economic support. With agencies working together to better situate families, fewer children might enter the child welfare or criminal justice systems. These agencies can also work together to provide post-incarceration services for both inmates and their families.

Social workers must have solid relationships with local prosecutors so that they can better advocate for clients. When prosecutorial injustice does occur, social workers will then know how better to track the misconduct and advocate for change.

Agencies can also educate community members on how to interact with the police and the courts. Listening forums allow communities to voice their concerns, fears, and anxiety about misconduct anywhere in the criminal justice system. They also allow social workers to document abuses and work for change within the entire system.

Cultural Competence in the Criminal Justice System

Policies must reinforce cultural competence throughout the criminal justice system. This includes hiring culturally competent management, supervisors, and direct workers, such as police and corrections officers. Cultural competence should be part of staff reviews across the criminal justice system and local review panels, composed primarily of community-selected representatives, who should rate the cultural competence of criminal justice organizations and have the power to change these organizations.

Infusing cultural competence throughout the criminal justice system will take time, be met with resistance, but is possible if there is a formal policy and significant reinforcement. For example, under the leadership of Leonard G. Dunston, MSW, former director of what was then the New York State Division for Youth, the state instituted Rites of Passage Programs for juveniles. These programs became a huge success in building self-esteem and creating stronger positive networks for young people. This African-centered approach has successfully been used with similar populations (Harvey and Coleman, 1997) and provides options for creating change in the criminal justice system.

SYSTEMIC ISSUES TO BE ADDRESSED

Substance Abuse Treatment

Policymakers must advocate for significant changes within options for substance abuse treatment. "In New York the cost of keeping a confined drug offender in prison is $30,000 a year compared to $2,700 to $3,600 per year for most outpatient drug programs and $17,000 to $20,000 per year for residential programs" (American Psychological Association, 1999, p. 2). Substance abuse treatment services should first be culturally competent and accessible. Second, individuals should be assessed for readiness for treatment. Third, treatment, when appropriate, should be explored as the first option prior to incarceration. Finally, substance abuse treatment should be more readily available to women and men with children.

Poverty and Discrimination

As long as there is poverty and discrimination in employment, African-American communities will have disproportionate numbers in the criminal justice system (Comer, 1985; Sampson, 1987). There must be greater emphasis on community and economic development that emphasizes employment with livable wages (Jenson and Howard, 1998). Community-based, risk-focused interventions, particularly for juveniles, can help prevent increases in juvenile crime (Hawkins and Catalano, 1992; Jenson and Howard, 1998).

Dealing with Family Violence

Just as substance abuse is a critical issue, so is the issue of family and domestic violence. As earlier stated, "For all correctional populations, men who reported abuse generally had been age 17 or younger when they suffered the abuse. Women, however, were abused as both juveniles and adults" (Harlow, 1999, p. 2). There must be more research on the linkages between family violence and the criminal justice system, particularly for women and juveniles. Domestic violence, also highly linked to the criminal justice system, must be researched and better understood as it relates to criminal justice (Harlow, 1999; Richie, 1996).

Family Programs

Comer (1985) and Hairston (1997) advocate for greater family programs in prison, such as parenting and other support groups. "Imprisonment disrupts normal family functioning and parent-child relationships and creates emotional distress, financial difficulties, social stigma and isolation, legal problems" (Hairston, 1997, p. 144). Family programs are particularly important as the average inmate is likely to be released from prison within two years (Schlosser, 1998). Currently, many faith- and community-based organizations provide some of these services. Social workers must work with these established programs to structure parenting and other support mechanisms to help reintroduce individuals back into society, creating a greater sense of interconnection.

PUBLIC POLICY ADVOCACY

Social justice cannot truly be achieved until social work recommits to changing the criminal justice system. Although there has been some acknowledgment of the criminal justice policy issues from social workers (NASW, 2001), the disparate treatment of African Americans and Latinos in the criminal justice system has received limited attention. The National Association of Blacks in Criminal Justice has provided great leadership in this area and the National Association of Black Social Workers has included criminal justice issues in their public policy institutes and conferences for several years. This concern needs to be expanded into greater policy advocacy.

A number of proposed laws could create changes and provide the basis for a specific policy action agenda. The Drug Sentencing Reform Act of 2001 (S.1874) was sponsored in the Senate by Senator Jeffrey Sessions (D-AL) to reduce the disparity between crack and powder cocaine sentencing and consider the role of the offender in sentencing. This act was referred to the Senate Committee on the Judiciary on December 20, 2001.

H.R. 1978, Major Drug Trafficking Prosecution Act of 2001 was sponsored in the House by Representative Maxine Waters (D-CA) to eliminate MMS for small time drug offenses. This Act was referred to the House Subcommittee on Health on June 1, 2001.

The Racial Profiling Prohibition Act of 2001 (H.R. 1907/H.R. 965), sponsored in the House by Representative Eleanor Holmes Norton (D-DC), will withhold federal highway funds from law enforcement organizations caught engaging in racial profiling. H.R. 1907 was referred to the House Subcommittee on Highways and Transit on May 18, 2001. H.R. 965 was referred to the House Subcommittee on Highways and Transit on March 9, 2001.

The End Racial Profiling Act of 2001 (H.R. 2074/S989), sponsored in the House by Representative John Conyers (D-MI) and in the Senate by Senator Russell Feingold (D-WI) prohibits racial profiling and increases accountability for racial profiling. H.R. 2074 was referred to the House Subcommittee on Crime on July 16, 2001. S.989 was referred to the Senate Committee on the Judiciary Subcommittee on Constitution on August 1, 2001.

The Law Enforcement Trust and Integrity Act of 2000 (H.R. 3927/H.R. 3981) was sponsored in the House by Representative John

Conyers (D-MI) to provide incentives for performance-based standards, to institute new national standards, and to include whistleblower protections. This act was referred to the House Subcommittee on Crime on March 31, 2000.

The Accuracy on Judicial Administration Act of 2000 (H.R. 4162/ H.R. 3623) was sponsored in the House by Representative Jesse Jackson Jr. (D-IL) to provide a seven-year moratorium on executions. H.R. 3623 was referred to the House Subcommittee on Crime on March 27, 2000. H.R. 4162 was referred to the same subcommittee on April 14, 2000.

The National Death Penalty Moratorium Act of 2001 (S.233/H.R. 1038), was sponsored in the Senate by Senator Russell Feingold (D-WI) to deal with racial disparities in death penalty implementation. S.233 was referred to the Subcommittee on Constitution, Federalism, and Property Rights on June 13, 2001. H.R. 1038 was referred to the House Subcommittee on Crime on April 19, 2001.

The Innocence Protection Act of 2001 (H.R. 912/S486) was sponsored by Representative William D. Delahunt (D-MA) and Senator Patrick J. Leahy (D-VT). The purpose of the act is to reduce the risk of executing an innocent person. Subcommittee hearings were held on H.R. 912 on June 18, 2002. S.486 was placed on the Senate Legislative Calendar under General Orders, Calendar No. 731. It is anticipated that this act will come to the floor in 2003.

The Second Chance Voting Rights Act of 2000 (H.R. 5158) was introduced in the House by Representative Juanita Millender-McDonald (D-CA) to "restore those rights to formerly incarcerated persons upon their unconditional release from state, federal, or District of Columbia prison and the completion of their sentence, including parole" (CBCF News, 2001, p. 15). This act was referred to the House Subcommittee on Crime on September 21, 2000.

These proposed acts provide concrete examples of legislation that social workers can lobby on behalf of to impact the criminal justice system. Advocacy for the above acts within states and on a federal level can make a difference.

LESSONS FROM OUR HISTORY

African-American social welfare history provides many opportunities to learn methods of intervention (Gabbidon, Greene, and Young,

2002). For example, Ida B. Wells-Barnett, our nation's first African-American probation officer (Bent-Goodley, 2001), provided a model for using an individual caseload to create a macro-level intervention. Wells-Barnett forfeited her salary to start the Negro Fellowship League (NFL). The League provided employment information, housing, literacy training, and counseling services. Janie Porter Barrett established the Virginia Industrial School for Colored Girls to provide counseling and moral guidance to teenage girls (Peebles-Wilkins, 1995; Peebles-Wilkins and Francis, 1990). The organization emphasized the importance of housing and teaching life and employment skills. Not only was Barrett able to pull together community support but her intervention was effective.

Both of these pioneers recognized the interrelationship of housing, community support, individual counseling, quality employment, and literacy training for those in the criminal justice system. These types of community-based alternatives provide examples of what can be done when the African-American community comes together with the resolve to creatively respond to criminal justice issues. More important, they are specific examples of why African Americans need to reach back and embrace the options posed through African-American social welfare history.

CONCLUSION

My introduction into the criminal justice system was largely a result of working as a social worker in child welfare and domestic violence. After monitoring juveniles' problems and watching the criminal justice system's approach to domestic violence, I came to realize that all social workers needed to know something about the criminal justice system. In this chapter, I have attempted to illuminate the policy issues related to criminal justice, articulate the disparity in treatment of African Americans, and provide an action agenda.

The criminal justice system is complex. It is recognized that along with an inmate rightfully convicted is a family suffering in pain and feeling victimized. The criminal justice system must first speak for them, first by changing their conditions and second by fairly punishing those who choose to hurt others.

On one level it is hard to sympathize with someone who has committed a crime. Yet we must be fair in our treatment. When one person's civil rights are violated, we all experience an injustice. Perhaps that is the most appropriate motivation for untangling the distortions in the web that has been woven.

REFERENCES

Alridge, D.P. and Daniels, M. (2001). Black violence and crime: A socio-historical structural analysis. In L.A. See (Ed.), *Violence as seen through a prism of color* (pp. 27-43). Binghamton, NY: The Haworth Press, Inc.

American Psychological Association (1999). American Psychological Association endorses reform of mandatory sentences. Available: <http://www.famm.org/index2.htm>.

Austin, J. and Coventry, G. (2001). *Emerging issues on privatized prisons* (NCJ Publication No. 181249). Washington, DC: Department of Justice.

Beck, A.J. and Harrison, P.M. (2001). *Prisoners in 2000* (NCJ Publication No. 188207). Washington, DC: Bureau of Justice Statistics.

Beck, A.J. and Mumola, C.J. (1999). *Prisoners in 1998* (NCJ Publication No. 175687). Washington, DC: Bureau of Justice Statistics.

Beckerman, A. (1994). Mothers in prison: Meeting the prerequisite conditions for permanency planning. *Social Work, 39,* 9-14.

Bent-Goodley, T.B. (2001). Ida B. Wells-Barnett: An uncompromising style. In I. Carlton-LaNey (Ed.), *African American leadership: An empowerment tradition in social welfare history* (pp. 87-98). Washington, DC: NASW Press.

Bilchik, S. (1999). *Minorities in the juvenile justice system.* Washington, DC: OJJDP.

Blumstein, A. (1982). On the racial disproportionality of United States prison population. *Journal of Criminal Law and Criminology, 73,* 1259-1282.

Blumstein, A. (1993). Racial disproportionality of U.S. prison populations revisited. *University of Colorado Law Review, 64,* 743-759.

Blumstein, A. (2001). Race and criminal justice. In N.J. Smelser, W.J. Wilson, and F. Mitchell (Eds.), *America becoming: Racial trends and their consequences* (Vol. 1) (pp. 21-31). Washington, DC: National Research Council.

Branigan, W. and Smith, L. (2001). Mentally ill need care, find prison: Without treatment, many cycle in and out of jail. *The Washington Post,* Al, A8-A9.

Bush-Baskette, S.R. (1998). The war on drugs as a war against black women. In S.L. Miller (Ed.), *Crime control and women: Feminist implications of criminal justice policy* (pp. 113-129). Thousand Oaks, CA: Sage.

CBCF News (2001). Representative Millender-McDonald champions voting rights for ex-inmates. *CBCF News, 3,* January 15.

Center for Mental Health Services (1995). *Double jeopardy: Persons with mental illnesses in the criminal justice system.* Rockville, MD: Department of Health and Human Services.

Chaiken, J.M. (2000, January). Crunching numbers: Crime and incarceration at the end of the millennium (NJC 180078). Washington, DC: National Institute of Justice.

Chandler, S.M. and Kassebaum, G. (1997). Meeting the needs of female offenders. In C.A. McNeece and A.R. Roberts (Eds.), *Policy and practice in the justice system* (pp. 159-180). Chicago: Nelson-Hall Publishers.

Cole, D. (1999). *No equal justice: Race and class in the American criminal justice system.* New York: The New Press.

Comer, J.P. (1985). Black violence and public policy. In L.A. Curtis and B. Moyers (Ed.), *American violence and public policy: An update of the National Commission on the causes and prevention of violence.* New Haven, CT: Yale University Press.

Congressional Quarterly (2000). *Issues in social policy: Selections from the CQ Researcher.* Washington, DC: Congressional Quarterly Press.

Conly, C. (1998). The women's prison association: Supporting women offenders and their families. Available: <http://ncjrs.org/txtfiles/172858.txt>, January 15, 2000.

Corcoran, K. and Shireman, C. (1997). M.S.W. education for the justice system: From the rehabilitative ideal to generalist practice. In C.A. McNeece and A.R. Roberts (Eds.), *Policy and practice in the justice system* (pp. 251-262). Chicago: Nelson-Hall Publishers.

Cose, E. (2000). America's prison generation. *Newsweek, 86* (November 13) (20), 40-46.

Crutchfield, R.D., Glusker, A., and Bridges, G.S. (1999). A tale of three cities: Labor markets and homicide. *Sociological Focus, 32,* 65-83.

Danner, M.J.E. (1998). Three strikes and it's women who are out: The hidden consequences for women of criminal justice policy reforms. In S.L. Miller (Ed.), *Crime control and women: Feminist implications of criminal justice policy* (pp. 1-14). Thousand Oaks, CA: Sage.

Dickey, W.J. and Hollenhorst, P. (1999). Three-strikes laws: Five years later. *Corrections Management Quarterly, 3,* 1-18.

Duke, L. (2000). Jury acquits four New York officers: Panel rules police acted reasonably in slaying of Amadou Diallo. *The Washington Post,* A1, A13.

Feinman, C. (1980). *Women in the criminal justice system.* New York: Praeger.

Fields, G. and Johnson, K. (2000). Crime at lowest point in 32 years. *The Washington Post,* January 16, F4-5.

Fullilove, R.E. (2000). *Killing our people: HIV/AIDS destroying our lives—charting our future.* Paper presented at the policy institute African American Social Workers and Social Policy: Leadership for the New Millennium, June 22, Howard University, Washington, DC.

Gabbidon, S.L., Greene, H.T., and Young, V.D. (Eds.) (2002). *African-American classics in criminology and criminal justice.* Thousand Oaks, CA: Sage.

Gibbs, J. and Bankhead, T. (2001). *Preserving privilege: California politics, propositions and people of color.* Westport, CT: Praeger.

Greenfield, L.A. and Snell, T.L. (1999). *Women offenders* (NCJ Publication No. 175688). Washington, DC: Bureau of Justice Statistics.

Hairston, C.F. (1997). Family programs in state prisons. In C.A. McNeece and A.R. Roberts (Eds.), *Policy and practice in the justice system* (pp. 143-158). Chicago: Nelson-Hall Publishers.

Harlow, C.W. (1999). *Prior abuse reported by inmates and probationers* (NCJ Publication No. 172879). Washington, DC: Bureau of Justice Statistics.

Harvey, A.R. and Coleman, A. (1997). An Afrocentric program for African American males in the juvenile justice system. *Child Welfare, 76,* 197-211.

Hawkins, D.F., Laub, J.H., Lauritsen, J.L., and Cothern, L. (2000). *Race, ethnicity, and violent juvenile offending* (OJJDP Publication No. 181202). Washington, DC: OJJDP.

Hawkins, J.D. and Catalano, K.F. (1992). *Communities that care.* San Francisco, CA: Jossey-Bass.

Henriques, Z.W. and Manatu-Rupert, N. (2001). Living on the outside: African-American women before, during, and after imprisonment. *Prison Journal, 81,* 6-20.

Hickman, T. (2000). *Criminal justice: Fighting for equity, fairness and justice in an unjust system.* Paper presented at the policy institute African American Social Workers and Social Policy: Leadership for the New Millennium, June 22, Howard University, Washington, DC.

Hill, R. (1997). *The strengths of African American families: Twenty-five years later.* Washington, DC: R&B Publishers.

Human Rights Watch and The Sentencing Project (1998). *Losing the vote: The impact of felony disenfranchisement laws in the United States.* Washington, DC: Author.

Isaac, A.R., Lockhart, L.L., and Williams, L. (2001). Violence against women in prisons and jails: Who's minding the shop? In L.A. See (Ed.), *Violence as seen through a prism of color* (pp. 129-145). Binghamton, NY: The Haworth Press, Inc.

Jenson, J.M. and Howard, M.O. (1998). Youth crime, public policy, and practice in the juvenile justice system: Recent trends and needed reforms. *Social Work, 43,* 324-334.

Johnson, J.G. (2001). Violence in prison systems: An African-American tragedy. In L.A. See (Ed.), *Violence as seen through a prism of color* (pp. 105-128). Binghamton, NY: The Haworth Press, Inc.

Jonson-Reid, M. and Barth, R.P. (2000). From placement to prison: The path to adolescent incarceration from child welfare-supervised foster or group care. *Children and Youth Services Review, 22,* 493-516.

Juszkiewicz, J. (2000). *Youth crime/adult time: Is justice served?* Washington, DC: Building Blocks for Youth.

Klockars, C.B., Ivkovich, S.K., Harver, W.E., and Haberfeld, M.R. (2000). *The measurement of police integrity* (NCJ Publication No. 181465). Washington, DC: Bureau of Justice Statistics.

Krivo, L.J. and Peterson, R.D. (1996). Extremely disadvantaged neighborhoods and urban crime. *Social Forces, 75,* 619-650.

Kurshan, N. (1999). *Women and imprisonment in the United States: History and current reality.* Available: <http://prisonactivist.org/women/women-and-imprisonment.html>, December 6.

Lane, C. (2002). Justices to rule on "three strikes" law: California's tough sentencing of repeat offenders called "cruel and unique." *The Washington Post,* November 6, A04.

Langan, P.A. (1985). Racism on trial: New evidence to explain the racial composition of prisons in the United States. *The Journal of Criminal Law and Criminology, 76,* 666-683.

Langan, P.A., Greenfeld, L.A., Smith, S.K., Durose, M.R., and Levin, D.J. (2001). *Contacts between police and the public: Findings from the 1999 national survey* (BJS Publication No. 184957). Washington, DC: Bureau of Justice Statistics.

Liebman, J.S., Fagan, J., and West, V. (2000). *A broken system: Error rates in capital cases, 1973-1995.* Available: <http://justice.policy.net/proactive/newsroom/release.vtml?id=18200>, January 1, 2002.

Locy, T. (1999). Like mother, like daughter: Why more young women follow their moms into lives of crime. *U.S. News and World Report, 127* (October 4), 18-21.

Lundman, R.J. (2001). *Prevention and control of juvenile delinquency* (Third edition). New York: Oxford University Press.

Mauer, M. (1999). *Race to incarcerate: The sentencing project.* New York: The New Press.

McDonald, J.M. and Chesney-Lind, M. (2001). Gender bias and juvenile justice revisited: A multiyear analysis. *Crime and Delinquency, 47,* 173-196.

McNeece, C.A. and Roberts, A.R. (Eds.) (1997). *Policy and practice in the justice system.* Chicago: Nelson-Hall Publishers.

Montgomery, L. (2002). Maryland governor-elect to rescind execution moratorium. *The Washington Post,* November 16, B01.

The Moratorium Campaign (2002a). Death penalty a deterrent? South has the highest murder rate—and the highest rate of executions. Available: <http://www.moratorium2000.org/facts/stats.lasso>.

The Moratorium Campaign (2002b). General statistics. Available: <http://www.moratorium2000.org/facts/stats.lasso>.

Mumola, C.J. (2000). *Incarcerated parents and their children* (NCJ 182335). Washington, DC: Bureau of Justice Statistics.

National Association of Social Workers (2001). *Social work speaks* (Fifth edition). *NASW policy statements, 2000-2003.* Washington, DC: Author.

Nelson-Zlupko, L., Kauffman, E., and Dore, M.M. (1995). Gender differences in drug addiction and treatment: Implications for social work intervention with substance abusing women. *Social Work, 40,* 45-54.

Peebles-Wilkins, W. (1995). Janie Porter Barrett and the Virginia Industrial School for Colored Girls: Community response to the needs of African-American children. *Child Welfare, 46,* 143-161.

Peebles-Wilkins, W. and Francis, E.A. (1990). Two outstanding black women in social welfare history: Mary Church Terrell and Ida B. Wells-Barnett. *Affilia, 5,* 87-100.

Poe-Yamagata, E. and Butts, J.A. (1996). *Female offenders in the juvenile justice system.* Washington, DC: OJJDP.

Richie, B.E. (1996). *Compelled to crime: The gender entrapment of battered black women.* New York: Routledge.

Richie, B.E. (2000). Exploring the link between violence against women and women's involvement in illegal activity. In B.E. Richie, K.T. Senin, and C.S. Widom (Eds.), *Research in women and girls in the justice system: Plenary papers of the 1999 Conference in Criminal Justice Research and Evaluation—Enhancing Policy and Practice Through Research,* Vol. 3 (pp. 1-14) (NCJ Publication No. 180973). Washington, DC: National Institute of Justice.

Roberts, A.R. (Ed.) (1997). *Social work in juvenile and criminal justice settings* (Second edition). Springfield, IL: Charles C. Thomas Publisher.

Russell, K.K. (1998). *The color of crime: Racial hoaxes, white fear, black protectionism, police harassment, and other macroaggressions.* New York: New York University Press.

Sampson, R.J. (1987). Urban black violence: The effect of male joblessness and family disruption. *American Journal of Sociology, 93,* 348-382.

Schlosser, E. (1998). The prison-industrial complex. *The Atlantic Monthly, 282,* 51-79.

The Sentencing Project (2000). *Reducing racial disparity in the criminal justice system: A manual for practitioners and policymakers.* Washington, DC: Author.

Snell, T.L. (2001). *Capital punishment 2000* (BJS Publication No. 190598). Washington, DC: Bureau of Justice Statistics.

Snyder-Joy, Z.K. and Carlo, T.A. (1998). Parenting through prison walls: Incarcerated mothers and children's visitation programs. In S.L. Miller (Ed.), *Crime control and women: Feminist implications of criminal justice policy* (pp. 130-150). Thousand Oaks, CA: Sage.

Spohn, C. and Holleran, D. (2000). The imprisonment penalty paid by young, unemployed black and Hispanic male offenders. *Criminology, 38,* 281-307.

Taifa, N. (in press). Social policy implications of racial disparities in the criminal justice system. In K.E. Davis and T.B. Bent-Goodley (Eds.), *The color of social policy.* Alexandria, VA: Council on Social Work Education.

Tewksbury, R., Erickson, D.J., and Taylor, J.M. (2000). Opportunities lost: The consequences of eliminating Pell Grant eligibility for correctional educational students. *Journal of Offender Rehabilitation, 31,* 43-56.

Van Wormer, K.S. and Bartollas, C. (2000). *Women and the criminal justice system.* Boston, MA: Allyn and Bacon.

Weich, R.H. and Angulo, C.T. (2000). *Justice on trial: Racial disparities in the American criminal justice system.* Washington, DC: Leadership Conference on Civil Rights.

Wilson, A.N. (1990). Black-on-black violence: The psychodynamics of black self-annihilation in service of white domination. New York: Africa World InfoSystems.

Young, D.S. and LoMonaco, S.W. (2001). Incorporating content on offenders and corrections into social work curricula. *Journal of Social Work Education, 37,* 475-492.

Chapter 9

Genetics: The Social Policy Implications for African Americans

Tricia B. Bent-Goodley

Increasingly, social workers are exploring the impact of advancements in genetics research. The Human Genome Project (HGP) will provide an opportunity for more targeted medical intervention, healthier and more nutritious meals, and more effective methods of fighting disease. Genetics information is already a big part of American life. Genetics data banks include pathology specimens, blood bank donations, newborn-screening samples, and, increasingly, forensic DNA data banks.

In February 2001 the human DNA sequence was decoded (Venter et al., 2001). References were quickly made to having found the blueprint of life and that this finding would form the basis of the medicine of the future. Although the HGP provided a new vision, it also spawned many ethical, legal, and civil rights issues to consider (Buchanan et al., 2000; Ross, 2001; Vastag, 2001; White, 2000). African Americans should be particularly concerned about how this new genetic information will be used (Bowman, 2000; Francis, 2001). Genetics has often been used to discriminate against and stigmatize African Americans. African-American social workers must be aware of the HGP and how it can affect African Americans both positively and negatively. The purposes of this chapter are twofold: (1) to analyze what the HGP means for social workers, and (2) to suggest a plan of action on how African Americans can impact the HGP.

The author wishes to thank Dr. Jean E. McEwen for her support of this chapter.

WHY AFRICAN AMERICANS SHOULD BE CONCERNED ABOUT GENETICS

African Americans have been regarded as genetically predisposed to be more aggressive, demonstrate athletic superiority, have a "greater intensity to pain, greater ability to tolerate manual labor, and lesser control of [their] emotions when compared to Whites" (Solomon, 1976, p. 156). At the same time, the explosion of genetics information poses significant opportunities for African Americans and not just for health reasons.

First, genetics has confirmed that life originated in Africa. This confirmation puts Africa at the center of analysis for the entire human species. "You can't understand human variation without Africa" (Dunston, 2001). In essence, we are "one human family over multiple generations" (Dunston, 2001). This finding should reinforce the significance and importance of Africa and African people to the world and stimulate thinking as to how people view themselves.

> The gene pool in Africa contains more variation than elsewhere, and that the genetic variation found outside of Africa contains only a subset of that found within the African continent. From a genetic perspective, all humans are therefore Africans, either residing in Africa or in recent exile. (Paabo, 2001, p. 2)

This assertion warrants a true dialogue around issues of race and culture, and honesty about the beginnings of civilization.

Second, the human genome sequence disproves all of the previous assertions that African Americans are genetically different from other groups. Differences in a person's ability to metabolize drugs is clustered according to genotype or genetic markers, not race (Bowman, 2000). Thus, the HGP diffuses separation based on race and confirms these distinctions as social and cultural phenomena (Bowman, 2000). These findings should further dispel the notion that African Americans are genetically inferior and that there is no scientific basis for calling any group of people inferior or superior.

Third, the human genome sequence provides an opportunity to address health disparities in new and exciting ways. Sickle cell disease, diabetes, and heart disease are among the diseases that disproportionately affect African Americans (USDHHS, 2001). Genetics information can allow physicians to create medical interventions targeted to meet the unique needs of a single individual; perhaps even finding cures or preventive measures.

Fourth, advanced knowledge of the human genome can allow African Americans to trace their lineage (Collins and McKusick, 2001). This advancement can give African Americans the opportunity to trace their lineage to a particular part or country of Africa. Although there is some disagreement as to the accuracy of this technology, the possibility of lineage tracing is exciting.

BACKGROUND

The HGP began in 1990 as a collaboration between the National Institute of Health (NIH) and the Department of Energy. The initial goals of the HGP were

1. to map and sequence the human genome,
2. map and sequence the genomes of importance,
3. map and sequence model organisms,
4. study the ethical, legal and social implications of genetic research,
5. train researchers,
6. develop technologies [to study functions of genes and sequence variation], and
7. transfer technologies to the private sector. (Jegalian, 2001, p. 1)

The current goals of the HGP focus primarily on the study of genetic variation. Former President Clinton proposed a $1 billion increase for the NIH to conduct biomedical research, largely to fund individual researchers. In 2001, NIH began its "focus on the following four themes: (1) exploiting the power of genomics, (2) reinvigorating clinical research, (3) harnessing the expertise of allied scientific and engineering disciplines that contribute to biomedical research, and (4) reducing disparities in health" (White House Office of the Press Secretary, 2000, p. 2).

Decoding the human genome sequence laid the foundation for further inquiry into the order, relationship, and patterns of variation (Lander et al., 2001). Advanced information on genetics allows scientists to "study genes themselves [as opposed to continuing to] study genes through people" (Dunston, 2001). Biological and social scientists have always sought to understand phenomena by seeking the commonality of conditions or events. Advanced genetics information changes this way of thinking by challenging scientists to understand variance. The genome teaches us that variance is actually the norm. "It forces us to rethink what we have been taught and find new ways of interpreting" (Dunston, 2001).

The HGP has made an effort to consider not just the biology of this new information but also the ethical and social implications of genetics research. This goal reinforces the importance of having diverse ethnic, professional, and economic stakeholders at the table to fully discuss the opportunities and challenges of genetics research. Social workers must be there to provide unique insights and advocate for those who could be harmed either by the implications of the new information or by the process of obtaining it.

EMERGING OPPORTUNITIES

Among the opportunities that may result from advances in genetics research are increased life expectancy, better quality of life, and closure on significant life issues through (1) enhanced screening and prevention, (2) more precise prediction, (3) enhanced pharmacogenomics, (4) better environmental outcomes, and (5) criminal justice implications.

Enhanced Screening and Prevention

Screening and prevention are also key outcomes of the HGP. Knowledge of genetic makeup and risks for disease gives physicians and patients advanced warnings of potential medical issues so that together they can act to prevent them. In addition to current prenatal screenings, fetuses can be screened for enzyme deficiencies, in many cases allowing them to be treated in utero. Carrier screening allows those with dormant genes that can be passed on without knowledge to be identified. Advanced genetics information allows scientists to further these types of screenings.

More Precise Prediction

With advanced genetics information, scientists can better classify some health conditions. Better classification can lead to a more precise diagnosis and possibly in a shorter time period (Collins and MuKusick, 2001). In essence, genetics information can allow physicians to better and more accurately diagnose disease. Better diagnosis leads inevitably to better targeting of the ailment and more effective treatment. For example, advanced genetics information can allow for more precise information in matching organ donors with transplant recipients. This opportunity can help save lives and provide people with a chance to better understand what is happening in their bodies, creating more informed decision making. These opportunities are critical to advancing medical interventions that are more effective and timely.

Enhanced Pharmacogenomics

Pharmacogenomics allows drugs to be tailored to the needs of the individual at the molecular level that is the source of the disease; such "gene-based designer drugs" (Collins and McKusick, 2001, p. 11) could be available as early as 2020. In 1998, almost $30 billion was spent on pharmacological research. Scientists will study genetic variation so that the effect of drugs on an individual can be determined. This opportunity may be particularly significant for the way we treat mental illness (McEwen, 2000), substance abuse (Nestler and Landsman, 2001), and even HIV/AIDS. Imagine being able to treat clients with a uniquely personal medication responding only to their individual needs. It could lessen negative reactions to medication and optimize the effectiveness of clinical interventions. Social workers must play a part in pharmacogenomics because it is often their responsibility to monitor those receiving medication for both physical and mental health reasons.

Environmental Outcomes

Advanced genetics information can help us find ways to better clean up toxic waste, identify pollutants, and treat pathogens in the environment. Genetics information can help in breeding healthier animals and providing more nutritious produce that is disease-free and less insect-infested. Advances in genetics knowledge can also support work on how to defend against biological and chemical warfare (Human Genome Management Information System, 2001). Having this knowledge is critical to saving lives and taking a proactive stance toward terrorist attacks.

Criminal Justice Implications

There are positive implications for genetics information in the area of criminal justice (Turman, 2001). Genetics has been used to identify victims, providing closure for family members. It has also been used to vindicate inmates on death row. Using DNA information in criminal justice can actually save innocent lives. Thus, genetics poses opportunities to right wrongs and protect individuals from experiencing injustice.

THE CHALLENGES

Although advances in genetics information will provide enormous opportunities for a better quality of life, there are also areas that warrant concern, particularly for African Americans.

Psychological Effects

Increased knowledge of genetics information could create a sense of undue stress and anxiety. For example, some individuals may feel hopeless or overwhelmed when they learn about a genetic anomaly and may lose sight of the ability to potentially change a negative outcome. New genetics information "could lead a person to lapse into unhealthy behavior out of feelings of helplessness" (Meadows, 2001, p. 1). Without proper counseling and followup care, individuals whose genetic risks are identified could become fearful. "The construction of ideology of spurious bases of genetic endowment foreshortens the powerful influence of the collective experience and reduce[s] that experience to something less than it should be" (Solomon, 1976, p. 160).

An individual's genetic diagnosis may also have implications for the larger family (Capron, 1994). For example, the individual may find out that she has a diagnosis that is actually a part of her family's genetic make-up. One must consider how the family might be impacted by such a discovery, especially considering that they did not seek the intervention. Therefore, issues of informed consent must take into account the potential psychological impact on families (Lewin, 2000; Patrinos and Drell, 1997).

An additional issue that connotes a possible psychological impact is that advanced genetics information can determine genetics "problems much greater in scope and significance" (McKusick, 1994, p. 628). As a result, it could "widen the gap between what we can diagnose and what we can treat" (McKusick, 1994, p. 628). In essence, it is possible that new genetics information could leave physicians with less information as to how to treat an ailment, particularly in the initial stages of identifying new discoveries. This must be considered as it relates to the psychological effect on patients.

Disparate Access to Medical Services

Lack of access to medical services is already a major issue for African Americans, people of color, and the poor (Collins and McKusick, 2001; Mehiman, 1999). It is unclear how these populations will be able to benefit when access to genetic information is limited by lack of cultural competence, geographic location, and financial constraints. One must also consider accessibility through over-the-counter prescriptions. For example, one can purchase pregnancy tests in supermarkets and corner stores. To what extent will this type of accessibility continue? For example, could the possibility of obtaining paternity tests at local supermarkets be an option in the future? These types of issues need to be explored as one looks at the complexity of accessibility. Simultaneously, the issue of what is appropriate for accessibility warrants discussion. The possibility that historically oppressed populations may not have equal access to genetics information is of grave concern.

Policy Loopholes

Current federal laws and policies are inadequate to protect Americans (Jeffords and Daschle, 2001; Zimmern, Emery, and Richards, 2001). The Health Insurance Portability and Accountability Act of 1996 (PL 104-191) provides protection against large health plans discriminating on the basis of genetics information. Yet, this policy does not include small health plans. In 2000, President Clinton initiated an Executive Order that prohibits civilian federal employees from having their genetic information collected or used. Currently, laws protect Americans against discrimination based on genetics information as it relates to privacy, confidentiality, employment, and health or life insurance discrimination (HGMIS, 2001). Over two dozen states have already instituted policies that will prohibit genetic discrimination in the workplace and in obtaining health insurance; however, there are no federal guidelines and protections in place in the other states (Collins and McKusick, 2001). This piecemeal approach to policymaking is not effective because it does not equally protect all Americans against genetics discrimination.

Family Planning Issues

Reproductive decision making and adoption, already complicated issues, can become even more challenging from advances in genetics. Although individuals can already request genetics information on the health of a fetus, new advances will broaden what can be tested, including determining a greater number of genetic predispositions with a fetus. The results could fuel more heated discussion about termination of pregnancies in these instances.

A second issue to consider is the impact of advanced genetics information on foster care and adoption. Certain genetic information might prevent foster parents and adoptive parents from being accepted as caregivers. At the same time, adoptive parents may request more advanced genetics information about children, potentially resulting in the decision not to adopt a child. While on one level, these types of decisions provide more information on preventive care, they have also been used to discriminate. Billings et al. (1994) found that families and couples were discriminated against in being able to adopt due to a genetics predisposition. For example, a couple received a letter from an adoption agency indicating the following: "We have decided, in your situation, not to proceed with your application because there is a fifty-fifty chance of your getting Huntington Disease" (p. 641). Noting that this type of discrimination has already taken place and that advanced genetics information will provide greater opportunities for identifying various genetics predispositions, policymakers must consider this issue very seriously.

Lack of Trust

Researchers will struggle with a lack of trust from African Americans regarding participation in research and necessary clinical trials (Capron, 1994; Francis, 2001). "Genetic issues tend to be perceived as perpetrators of negative racial stereotypes and unseemingly pessimistic determinisms in regards to what Blacks can achieve. Rarely is genetics considered to be a source of understanding and effective helping" (Solomon, 1976, p. 140).

Capron (1994) documents specific examples of employment discrimination against African Americans as a result of sickle cell testing only two decades ago. He further documents how many states adopted mandatory screening laws of newborns for phenylketonuria (PKU), a "condition that causes mental retardation unless the affected child is placed on a special diet that severely restricts intake of phenylalanine" (p. 631). Although parents are mandated to screen for this condition, they are not mandated to place the child found with PKU on a special diet. As a result, one questions both the policies and the intention of policymakers in this decision.

With this perception of health care and scientists, it will be a challenge to engage African Americans in clinical trials and health interventions. Although the HGP has made an effort to engage researchers of color and has made ethics a cornerstone issue of the project, there is continued difficulty in securing researchers of color and implementing genetics research from a culturally competent perspective. The Howard University National Human Genome Center has made significant progress in this area.

IMPLICATIONS

Advanced genetics information provides significant opportunities for responding both to health care needs and to societal discrimination against African Americans. Social workers are keenly positioned to serve as policy advocates, community organizers, and educators. There are a number of manners in which social workers, particularly African-American social workers, can address the challenges just outlined and embrace the possibilities of human genome research.

Increasing Mental Health and Community-Based Services

As the largest provider of mental health services in the country (Vallianatos, 2002), social workers are uniquely positioned to provide education and genetics counseling. First, social workers can provide clinical services for those who are directly or indirectly affected by obtaining genetics information. Second, social workers often monitor individuals on medication prescribed by psychiatrists. With psychiatrists prescribing medication uniquely tailored to the individual, social workers can more readily focus on the individual's social, cognitive behavioral issues. Third, social workers can provide clients with information and necessary referrals once they obtain genetics information. They can organize community-based events that educate the public on genetics. Social workers can also monitor research and serve as liaisons for community-based research. In addition, social workers can advocate for greater community participation in serving on ethics review committees (Moulton, 2001), clinical trial's boards and other research (Wertz and Gregg, 2000). Lastly, in order for social workers to provide such services, schools of social work need to provide more information on genetics through both continuing education and academic course work.

Advocacy for Access

It is particularly critical that social workers, reflecting on the health disparities of African Americans, advocate for equal access. By monitoring genetics services and research, social workers are clearly positioned to identify disparate treatment and unequal access. Once identified, social workers are obligated to find creative solutions to address inequality.

Legislative Advocacy

Social workers must advocate for privacy and confidentiality laws that protect all citizens and especially African Americans and other people of color. Advocating for federal and state policies that ensure that genetics information cannot be used as a basis to discriminate in family planning, employment, and life and health insurance are key areas for immediate intervention. The Universal Declaration of the Human Genome and Human Rights clearly prohibits discrimination based on genetics characteristics and information (Jeffords and Daschle, 2001). Any legislation adopted should conform to these standards.

The Genetic Information Nondiscrimination in Health Insurance Act of 2001 (S. 382) was sponsored by Senator Olympia J. Snowe (R-ME) to prohibit discrimination in health insurance based on genetics information. The bill was referred to the Committee on Health, Education, Labor, and Pensions on February 15, 2001. Hearings were held on S.382 in the Senate Committee on Health, Education, Labor, and Pensions on February 13, 2002. There has been no further follow-up. Senator Snowe also introduced the Genetic Information Nondiscrimination Act of 2002 (S.1995). This act will prohibit genetics discrimination in employment and health insurance. The act was referred to the Senate Committee on Health, Education, Labor, and Pensions on March 6, 2002, with no additional follow-up.

Although important steps, these bills do not provide adequate protection for other discriminatory possibilities, particularly in the areas of family planning, employment, and health insurance discrimination, nor do they address equal access and protections related to genetic screening. In addition, policymakers must reexamine the notion of providing health care that is not linked to employment, ensuring universal health care for every citizen, and address the moral mandates related to advances in genetics information (Kiefer, 2001; Nicholas, 2001). While considering this issue, one must also consider who decides what is moral or immoral and how spirituality fits into deciding this question. African Americans and social workers must be a part of this important dialogue.

Addressing Discrimination in Research

Social workers must not only be a part of genetics research, they must be active participants and leaders. African-American social workers are positioned to both coordinate and protect African Americans who participate in genetics research. Greater emphasis should be placed on serving as principal investigators and establishing centers and institutes, such as the one at Howard University, that provide culturally competent genetics research. There should be an increase in funding to define cultural competence as it relates to genetics research and intervention. Such research should lend a particular focus toward finding solutions to health disparities in the African-American community.

CONCLUSION

This chapter has highlighted the strengths and challenges of genetics research. The key recommendations are (1) to increase access to genetics information, (2) promote culturally competent genetics research that includes African Americans serving as principal investigators, (3) ensure privacy and confidentiality through federal, state, and agency policy, and (4) increase the role of social work in providing community-based mental health services that include advanced knowledge of genetics. Working with researchers and collaborating with genetics-based organizations can further protect African Americans and the larger public as advances in genetics open up new opportunities. The roles of advocate and community educator are thus critical elements of today's social work practice in an age of advanced genetic exploration.

REFERENCES

Billings, P.R., Kohn, M.A., de Cuevas, M., Beckwith, J., Alper, J.S., and Natowicz, M.R. (1994). Discrimination as a consequence of genetic testing. In T.L. Beauchamp and L. Walters (Eds.), *Contemporary issues in bioethics* (Fourth edition) (pp. 637-643). Belmont, CA: Wadsworth.

Bowman, J.E. (2000). Anthropology: From bones to the human genome. *Annals of the American Academy of Political and Social Science, 568,* 140-154.

Buchanan, A., Brock, D.W., Daniels, N., and Wikler, D. (2000). *From chance to choice: Genetics and justice.* New York: Cambridge University Press.

Capron, A.M. (1994). Which ills to bear? Reevaluating the threat of modern genetics. In T.L. Beauchamp and L. Walters (Eds.), *Contemporary issues in bioethics* (Fourth edition) (pp. 629-636). Belmont, CA: Wadsworth.

Collins, F.S. and McKusick, V.A. (2001). Implications of the Human Genome Project for medical science. *Journal of the American Medical Association, 285,* 540-544.

Dunston, L. (2001). Genomic research on the African Diaspora: Implications for minority health. Paper presented at The Human Genome Project Conference: The Challenges and Impact of Human Genome Research for Minority Communities, November 9, Zeta Phi Beta National Education Foundation, Washington, DC.

Francis, C.K. (2001). Medical ethos and social responsibility in clinical medicine. *Journal of Urban Health, 78,* 29-45.

Human Genome Management Information System (2001). *Genomics and its impact on medicine and society: A 2001 primer.* Washington, DC: Department of Energy.

Jeffords, J.M. and Daschle, T. (2001). Political issues in the genome era. *Science, 291* (February 16), 1249-1251.

Jegalian, K. (2001). *Genetics: The future of medicine* (NIH Publication No. 00-4873). Washington, DC: National Institute of Health.

Kiefer, F. (2001). Bioethics: Toughest policy calls of era. *Christian Science Monitor, 93,* 180-181.

Lander, E.S., Linton, L.M., Birren, B., Nusbaum, C., Zody, M.C., Baldwin, J., et al. (2001). Initial sequencing and analysis of the human genome. *Nature, 409,* 860-921.

Lewin, T. (2000). Boom in gene testing raises questions on sharing results. *The New York Times,* July 21, B10.

McEwen, J.E. (2000). *Social policy issues of genetics research: Twenty-first century challenges.* Paper presented at the policy institute of African-American Social Workers and Social Policy: Leadership for the New Millennium, June 23, Howard University, Washington, DC.

McKusick, V.A. (1994). The Human Genome Project: Plans, status, and applications in biology and medicine. In T.L. Beauchamp and L. Walters (Eds.), *Contemporary issues in bioethics* (Fourth edition) (pp. 622-629). Belmont, CA: Wadsworth.

Meadows, M. (2001). Genetic testing can lead to fear of stigmatization. Available: <http://www.omhrc.gov/ctg/ct-15.htm>.

Mehlman, M.J. (1999). How will we regulate genetic enhancement? *Wake Forest Law Review, 34,* 671-714.

Moulton, D. (2001). No public voice in genetics research? *Canadian Medical Association Journal, 165,* 200-213.

Nestler, E.J. and Landsman, D. (2001). Learning about addiction from the genome. *Nature, 409,* 834-835.

Nicholas, B. (2001). Exploring a moral landscape: Genetic science and ethics. *Hypatia, 16,* 45-64.

Paabo, S. (2001). The human genome and our view of ourselves. *Science, 291,* (February 16) 1219-1220.

Patrinos, A. and Drell, D.W. (1997). Introducing the human genome project: Its relevance, triumphs, and challenges. *The Judge's Journal, 36,* 3-12.

Ross, L.F. (2001). Ethical and policy issues in genetic testing. *Pancreatology, 1,* 576-580.

Solomon, B.B. (1976). *Black empowerment: Social work in oppressed communities.* New York: Columbia University Press.

Turman, K.M. (2001). *Understanding DNA evidence: A guide for victim service providers* (OJP Publication No. 185690). Washington, DC: U.S. Department of Justice.

U.S. Department of Health and Human Services (2001). *Mental health: Culture, Race, and Ethnicity: A supplement to Mental Health: A Report of the Surgeon General.* Rockville, MD: U.S. Department of Health and Human Services, Substance Abuse and Mental Health Services Administration, Center for Mental Health Services.

Vallianatos, C. (2002). Clark urges more funds for disaster. *NASW News, 47,* 1.

Vastag, B. (2001). Experts wrestle with social, ethical implications of human genome research. *Journal of the American Medical Association, 285,* 721-723.

Venter, J.C., Adams, M.D., Myers, E.W., Li, P.W., Mural, R.J., Sutton, G.G., Smith, H.O., et al. (2001). The sequence of the human genome. *Science, 291,* 1304-1351.

Wertz, D. and Gregg, R. (2000). Genetics services in a social, ethical and policy context: A collaboration between consumers and providers. *Journal of Medical Ethics, 26,* 261-266.

White, G.B. (2000). What we may expect from ethics and the law. *American Journal of Nursing, 100,* 114-118.

White House Office of the Press Secretary (2000). *The human genome project: Benefiting all humanity.* March 14. Washington, DC: Author.

Zimmern, R., Emery, J., and Richards, T. (2001). Putting genetics in perspective. *British Medical Journal, 322,* 1005-1007.

Chapter 10

A Policy Action Agenda

Tricia B. Bent-Goodley

This book has focused on solutions and recommendations to address the pervasive racism and discrimination that continues against African Americans (Daniels, 2001). Although there was an effort to include diverse perspectives and issues, greater emphasis was placed on considering options toward empowerment. The focus of this endeavor was not to list all of the policy issues but instead to challenge social workers, particularly African Americans, to be more engaged in planned change in the policy arena. For a more comprehensive list of various policy issues and their impact on people of African ancestry, one can examine the policy agenda developed by the Million Family March Committee (Million Family March, 2000). African Americans and social workers need to view themselves as individuals that are powerful and comfortable with wielding power to affect change (Hasenfeld, 1992). The following recommendations form the basis of a policy action agenda rooted in the perspective that social workers are powerful in their ability to inform and create change.

Political Empowerment

African-American social workers should use their knowledge and skills to help communities become empowered through the policy process. Solomon (1976) defines empowerment as "a process whereby persons who belong to a stigmatized social category throughout their lives can be assisted to develop and increase skills in the exercise of interpersonal influence and the performance of valued social roles" (p. 6). A false notion that social workers empower clients exists; when in fact, clients empower themselves. Social workers help people learn how to empower themselves so that they can exercise their own interpersonal influence to create change in their individual circumstance and larger environment. To date, there has been a limited emphasis on training African Americans to exercise their political clout. As changing demographics are on the horizon, it is even more important that African Americans are politically and economically empowered to influence change. Such efforts should begin early. For example, social workers can organize grade school children to advocate for improved public education. Human service administrators can encourage staff to document issues in the community for the purpose of advocacy. These are small steps but nonetheless important opportunities to wield political strength.

Development of a Task-Centered Organization

A Task-Centered Organization (TCO) should be established to bring the various African-American organizations together to create a policy agenda. There are notable efforts to inform African Americans about public policy through organizations such as the Joint Center for Political and Economic Studies. Yet the role of African-American social workers has been limited. A TCO, defined as a time-limited, outcome-focused entity, could be established that brings together traditional and grassroots leadership on an equal basis. TCOs can focus on achieving specific outcomes for a selected period of time. Thus TCOs allow for less jockeying for power and political shifting and more time for addressing challenges with an outcome-based focus.

Leadership Development and Change

Elders play a critical role in the African-American community. Without their guidance and wisdom, the community would crumble. Simultaneously, there must be a real transfer of power of leadership in the African-American community; one must consider how leaders are selected. Are they sanctioned by the same individuals in power to forward the same agenda? Or do they have the support of grassroots membership interested in results through an ethical and culturally grounded process? If we are to advance a policy agenda, there must be a shift in power.

Pooling Our Resources

When one considers the amount of money spent on attending conferences each year—sorority, fraternity, professional, civic—it becomes clear that there is a significant amount of money being spent
by African Americans. There are also significant resources being utilized toward the success of these endeavors, such as staffing, volun-
teers, and money expended. Many individuals are attending multiple
conferences and while the information is plentiful, as a community
we continue to diversify our resources and energy instead of collectively coordinating them. African-American organizations could better
pool resources for more optimal responses by coordinating conferences together. For example, if two like-minded organizations came
together and integrated their conferences the benefits would be mutu-
ally beneficial: (1) politicians pay greater attention to larger numbers
of constituents; (2) duplication of effort would be avoidable; (3) the
policy agenda would be more diverse and developed from a more collective perspective; and (4) a more efficient utilization of human capital would occur. Cost and revenue-sharing agreements could be developed to meet the needs of both organizations. The primary outcome
from this endeavor is to pool financial, social, and human resources
for a more productive outcome and use of energy.

Look to African-American Social Welfare History

African-American social welfare history is rich in examples of
how African Americans were able to do, as progressive era pioneer
Nannie Helen Burroughs said, "the wholly impossible" with far less
resources than African Americans have today. Mary McCloud
Bethune's Black Cabinet informed major public policy for African
Americans on a federal level. Leugenia Burns Hope established
Neighborhood Health Centers that also provided the basis of advocacy on tough issues, such as police misconduct, better transportation, and educational systems. These ancestors, and so many like
them, have paved the way and yet the full extent of their contributions
is unknown. The National Association of Black Social Workers,
(NABSW) National Academy for African-Centered Social Work promotes learning about African-American social welfare pioneers through
an assignment called the Intellectual Biography developed by Afri-

can-American social welfare history scholar, Dr. Iris B. Carlton-LaNey (Carlton-LaNey, 1990). This assignment has been adopted for all policy students at Howard University School of Social Work. Every school of social work should have such an assignment to better educate social workers, of all racial and ethnic groups, about the contributions of African Americans and other people of color to the profession of social work. African-American organizations should also better support this type of scholarship by funding historical projects of this kind. African-American social welfare history creates the ability to build on the strengths of African-American achievement as opposed to focusing on limitations.

Entrepreneurship and Economic Empowerment

As Schiele (2000) and Jewell (1988) note, there can be no political power without economic power. If a social worker helps clients to empower themselves, then African Americans, as part of that agenda, should be taught how to engage in entrepreneurship and create jobs versus continuing to teach social workers how to inhabit jobs (Bent-Goodley, 2001). Entrepreneurship is a key form of empowerment for African-American social workers. As heads of institutions, African-American social work entrepreneurs can establish greater policy networks, create agency policies that truly help clients empower themselves, and provide real economic opportunities for individual and community development.

The International Context

People of African ancestry must see themselves in an international context and not as small communities or solely American citizens.

> The time is past due for us to internationalize the problems of Afro-Americans. We have been too slow in recognizing the link in the fate of Africans with the fate of Afro-Americans. We have been too unknowing to understand and too misdirected to ask our African brothers and sisters to help us mend the chain of our heritage. (Breitman, 1967, pp. 122-123)

In 1972, the NABSW stated that they would no longer use the term "minority," as people of African ancestry compose the majority of people in the world (*St. Louis American,* 1979). When one understands the connection to Africa and the cultural traditions that continue to be a part of the daily activities of many people of African ancestry today, then it becomes even more apparent that people of African ancestry are more powerful when connected than divided.

The Spiritual Connection

Although it could be argued that the policy arena is not connected to the spiritual world, from an African-centered perspective spirituality cannot be separated from the material world, even within social policy (Schiele, 2000). The early Egyptians developed the earliest recorded social welfare system based on spiritual principles. If one sees advocacy and exerting influence as a part of a spiritual obligation and commitment, then one is more likely to function ethically and with integrity. Making decisions that respect people as spiritual beings, not persons of color, women, or other socially designated categories, will result in more equitable treatment.

An Ethical Code of Conduct for Policy Practice

African Americans must embrace policy practice as an avenue that can create opportunities for individual and community empowerment. As such, African-American social workers should be encouraged to utilize at least five criteria when considering policy practice (Chipungu, 1997; Schiele, 1997):

1. Policies must ensure collective advancement rather than highlighting individual deficits.
2. Policies must respect people as spiritual beings instead of devaluing or overvaluing material possessions.
3. Policies must ensure equal distribution and access for all citizens instead of encouraging individuals to simply survive on their own merits.
4. Policies should facilitate respect for interdependence instead of the self-interest of a few.

5. Policies should be formulated based on the inherent goodness of individuals rather than viewing people from a deficit perspective.

These criteria do not suggest that African Americans cannot be political; however, it does assert that there should be an ethical code of conduct that shapes their decision making and activity.

Conclusion

Social policy provides African Americans with multiple avenues of influence from formulating and analyzing policy, to lobbying for or against a policy, to wielding influence in the policy implementation process. One of our greatest African-American social welfare pioneers, Ida B. Wells-Barnett, states:

> Eternal vigilance is the price of liberty, and it does seem to me that notwithstanding all these social agencies and activities there is not that vigilance which should be exercised in the preservation of our rights. This leads me to wonder if we are not well satisfied to be able to point to our wonderful institutions with complacence and draw the salaries connected therewith, instead of being alert as the watchman on the wall. (Duster, 1970, p. 415)

African Americans must be the "watchman on the wall"—always fighting for truth, equality, and justice and not resting until all three become a reality.

REFERENCES

Bent-Goodley, T.B. (2001). Defining and conceptualizing social work entrepreneurship. *Journal of Social Work Education, 38,* 291-302.

Breitman, G. (1967). *The last year of Malcolm X: The evolution of a revolutionary.* New York: Merit Publishers.

Carlton-LaNey, I. (1990). The intellectual biography: A mechanism for integrating historical content. *Arete, 15,* 46-51.

Chipungu, S.S. (1997). A value based policy framework. In J.E. Everett, S.S. Chipungu, and B.R. Leashore (Eds.), *Child Welfare: An Africentric perspective* (pp. 290-305). Rutgers, NJ: State University of Rutgers Press.

Daniels, L.A. (Ed.) (2001). *The state of black America 2001.* New York: National Urban League.

Duster, A.M. (Ed.) (1970). *Crusade for justice: The autobiography of Ida B. Wells.* Boston, MA: Beacon Press.

Hasenfeld, Y. (1992). Power in social work practice. In Y. Hasenfeld (Ed.), *Human services as complex organizations* (pp. 259-275). Thousand Oaks, CA: Sage.

Jewell, K.S. (1988). *Survival of the black family: The institutional impact of United States social policy.* New York: Praeger.

Million Family March (2000). *The national agenda: Public policy issues analyses and programmatic plan of action 2000-2008.* Washington, DC: Author.

Schiele, J.H. (1997). An Afrocentric perspective on social welfare philosophy and policy. *Journal of Sociology and Social Welfare, 24,* 21-39.

Schiele, J.H. (2000). *Human services and the Afrocentric paradigm.* Binghamton, NY: The Haworth Press, Inc.

Solomon, B.B. (1976). *Black empowerment: Social work in oppressed communities.* New York: Columbia University Press.

St. Louis American (1979). Social workers shun term "minority". June 14.

Index